Henry Paton

Papers about the rebellions of 1715 and 1745

Henry Paton

Papers about the rebellions of 1715 and 1745

ISBN/EAN: 9783337209971

Printed in Europe, USA, Canada, Australia, Japan

Cover: Foto ©ninafisch / pixelio.de

More available books at **www.hansebooks.com**

PAPERS ABOUT

THE REBELLIONS

of 1715 and 1745

Edited, from the Original Manuscripts,

with Introduction and Notes, by

HENRY PATON, M.A.

COLLIGITE FRAGMENTA

NE SHS PEREANT

EDINBURGH

Printed at the University Press by T. and A. Constable

for the Scottish History Society

1893

I

A JOURNALL OF SEVERALL OCCURRENCES in 1715, by PETER CLARKE.

II

EIGHT LETTERS by WILLIAM NICOLSON, D.D., Bishop of Carlisle, to the ARCHBISHOP OF YORK, 1716

III

LEAVES FROM THE DIARY of JOHN CAMPBELL an Edinburgh Banker in 1745

INTRODUCTION

The Jacobite rebellions in Scotland in 1715 and 1745 still retain an interest and even a fascination for many readers of history. Much has been written, especially about the '45, which was organised and led by Prince Charlie in person, but any details regarding either of these important episodes in the life of Scotland can never be unwelcome. The three following short contributions to the subject, two relating to the less known insurrection of 1715, and the third to that of 1745, may therefore possess some interest.

I

The first is a journal of some of the proceedings of what may be called the English division of the Rebel army in 1715, being that portion of the insurrectionary force which operated in the north of England, and which, by a remarkable coincidence, met its fate at Preston in Lancashire on the very day the battle of Sherrifmuir was fought, and Inverness Castle was retaken by the friends of the Hanoverian dynasty in Scotland.

John, eleventh Earl of Mar, had collected a considerable army in the Highlands of Scotland in the interests of the Chevalier, and was making his way southwards when he was threatened by a force under the Duke of Argyll on behalf of King George. To create a diversion he sent a party of Highlanders under Brigadier Mackintosh of Borlum across the Firth of Forth, who were also to form a nucleus for the gathering of the Jacobites in the southern counties. Having, in spite of several English gunboats, made the passage of the Forth and landed near Cockenzie, Mackintosh threatened an attack upon Edinburgh, and entrenched himself in Leith. But he was immediately obliged, by the arrival of a part of Argyll's army, to retire into East Lothian.

Already a body of Jacobites had taken the field in Northumberland under the leadership of Thomas Foster, M.P. for that county, whose principal supporter was the Earl of Derwentwater. From them Mackintosh now received an invitation to join forces at Kelso, and he resolved to comply with the request. Crossing the Lammermoor Hills by Longformacus, and proclaiming the Pretender at Duns, he reached Kelso on 22d October, where Foster awaited him. Of the Scottish Lowland Lords, however, only Kenmure, Winton, and Carnwath cast in their lot with the Earl of Mar's enterprise.

From Kelso the united rebel force was obliged to march on the 27th, owing to the arrival on the opposite side of the Tweed of an English army under General Carpenter. Proceeding by Jedburgh, Hawick, and Langholm, it entered England on 1st November. Our journalist fell in with the expedition on the following day, and thenceforth presents us with a diurnal of its proceedings with apparently the fidelity of an eye-witness. He records the incidents of the marches from Penrith to Appleby, thence to Kendal, Kirkby Lonsdale, and Lancaster; the conduct of the Highlanders and officers at these places and on the way, and the names and ultimate fortunes of the very few who joined them. He also notes the march to the fatal town of Preston, and in a short additional postscript to his narrative gives a very brief account of the fighting there. He notes the incident of the erasing of the name of 'Queen Anne' and the 'Princess Sophia,' from the Common Prayer Book used in the church at Lancaster, and the substituting for these in a print-like script of the words 'King James' and the 'King's mother.' This he says was done by Mr. Paul, a clergyman of the Church of England, who, according to Patten's account, joined the rebels here; but who, according to our journalist, came with the Earl of Derwentwater. Patten also relates a similar freak perpetrated by 'one Mr. Guin, who went into the churches on their way and scratched out his Majesty King George's name and placed the Pretender's so nicely that it resembled print very much and the alteration could scarce be perceived.'[1] But as he relates this of Mr. Guin before and when they came to Kirkby Lonsdale, there is not necessarily any discrepancy in our journalist saying that Mr. Paul did the same at Lancaster.

The narrative is written in the form of a letter, and Peter Clarke, the writer, describes himself as clerk to Mr. Craikenthorp, attorney at law in Penrith. He had been but one month in this service when the rebels came. He pays just tribute to the mild behaviour of the Highlanders and the rest of the rebel army towards the inhabitants of the districts and towns through which they passed, and, indeed, contrasts it somewhat strongly with the conduct of King George's troops towards the loyal inhabitants of Preston.

The Manuscript Narrative is a thin quarto of sixteen closely written pages in the Laing Collection of Manuscripts in the University Library of Edinburgh, and from a note on the MS. by the late Mr. David Laing it would appear that he purchased it at the sale of the library of Mr. George Chalmers. After it had been put in type it was discovered to have been already printed by Dr. S. H. Ware, in vol. v. of the Publications of the Chetham Society. But as the text is there broken up into numerous short sections, and interspersed with narrative and comments by the editor, rendering it difficult to extricate Peter Clarke's own story, it has been thought well to reprint from the original in continuous form this narrative, which deals with so important an event in Scottish history.

---

[1] *History of the Late Rebellion*, p. 87.

II

The second of these three contributions to the history of
the Rebellions is a series of eight letters written by William
Nicolson, D.D., Bishop of Carlisle, the author of the *Historical
Library*, and other works, who afterwards became Bishop
of Derry in Ireland, and had just been appointed Archbishop of Cashel when he died.   From internal evidence it
appears they were written to Sir William Dawes, who was
Archbishop of York from 1713 to 1724.   The letters deal
chiefly with the trial of the Scottish prisoners taken at and
after the battle of Sheriffmuir, which was fought on 13th
November 1715.

It having been considered inexpedient by the Court to try
the prisoners in Scotland, Carlisle was selected as the English
town nearest to Scotland, and to the friends of the prisoners,
and a Commission of Oyer and Terminer was issued for the
trial to several English judges, Barons Tracy, Price, and
Scrope, with Chief Baron Smith of Scotland, to whom were
also joined the local justices.   With their proceedings the
letters are for the most part engaged, and as no detailed
account of these appears to have been published hitherto
they are of the greater interest.   The change of venue was
indeed resented in Scotland as an infringement of the Union,
and eminent legal advice was tendered to the prisoners not to
plead.   But other counsels prevailed, and as the judges were
disposed to clemency all went well.   Of sixty-six prisoners
carried to Carlisle, Peter Rae informs us that thirty-four were
liberated before being brought to trial, and of the rest, who
all pleaded guilty, twenty-four were sentenced to death, but
no day was ever fixed for their execution, and the others were
never sentenced at all.   He further tells us that one of those
liberated, John Paton of Grandhome in Aberdeenshire, was so
impressed with the clemency showed to them that he 'made a

famous speech in praise and commendation of his Majesty, King George's mercifull disposition, which, he said, he had oftentimes heard of, but now felt, to his utmost joy and gratitude; and that eye had not seen nor ear heard the like before, but that he and others were living witnesses thereof; which he said for himself, and he thought all the rest would assent to it; wishing his Majesty and his royal issue long life and that he might ever be the darling of his people.'[1]

The original letters are in the British Museum. A selection of Bishop Nicolson's Correspondence was published in 1809, by John Nicols, in two volumes 8vo, and is most interesting and useful for the period over which the letters extend, 1683-1727. But those now printed are not included in that work.

III

The third instalment relates to the rebellion of 1745, and consists of extracts from the business diary of an Edinburgh banker, during the period of Prince Charlie's stay in that town. Mr. John Campbell, who kept the diary, was connected with the family of Breadalbane. He was first a writer in Edinburgh, and was appointed in 1732 Assistant Secretary of the Royal Bank of Scotland there. Two years later he became second cashier, and in July 1745 was advanced to the position of principal cashier of the Bank, which he held till his death in 1777.

The extracts from the Diary begin on 14th September, the day after Prince Charlie's army had passed the Forth at the Fords of Frew, and when but two days' march now lay between it and the capital. All was alarm, and that day and the next saw the valuables and money of the Bank transferred to the Castle for safety. And just in time, as on the 16th the Highlanders were at the gates, and the town clamouring for surrender. For two days the valour of volunteers and troopers had been the hope and admiration of the citizens, but it oozed

---

[1] *History of the Late Rebellion*, p. 382.

away, without a blow, as the Highlanders drew near, and while
the troopers ignominiously fled in the ' Canter o' Coltbrig,' the
volunteers made haste to disarm and place themselves in the
position of non-combatants. A nominal resistance was offered
by the gates being kept shut, but by daylight on the 17th the
town was in the hands of the Rebels.

To avoid the Castle guns, Prince Charlie led his army round
to Duddingston, and disposing the main body in the valleys
below Arthur's Seat, he took possession of Holyrood Palace
and established his Court there. With the exception of the
two days during which he was absent at the battle of Preston-
pans (fought on 21st September) the Prince made Holyrood
his residence till the end of October.

During this time frequent demands were made upon Mr.
Campbell for money, which were generally complied with after
consultation with such of the directors of the Bank as were
available. This obliged him to make visits both to the Castle
and to Holyrood. He had numerous meetings with Mr. John
Murray of Broughton, the Prince's Secretary, and others at the
Prince's Court, and some of these appear to have been of an
agreeable and social character. By the 1st of November the
last of the Highlanders had left Edinburgh, and a fortnight
later regular troops having been drafted in, the Bank doors
were re-opened and business resumed. With the retransport-
ing of the Bank property from the Castle on the 23d Mr.
Campbell's concern with the Rebellion terminates.

These extracts also give some interesting information about
the habits of the time. They were made and printed for
private circulation in 1881. But as only twenty copies in all
were printed they are practically as unknown as if they had
remained in their original manuscript form. The Council
therefore decided to avail themselves of the kind permission
accorded to them by the Royal Bank of Scotland to reprint
the narrative for the benefit of the members of the Society.

I.

A JOURNALL of Severall Occurrences from 2d November 1715, in the Insurrection (began in Scotland) and concluded at Preston in Lancashire, on November 14, MDCCXV., kept by Peter Clarke.

Sir,—On Wednesday the second day of November one thousand seaven hundred and fifteen, the then high sherriff of Cumberland assembled the *posse comitatus* on Penrith Fell, Viscount Loynsdale being there as commander of the malitia of Westmoreland, Cumberland, and Northumberland, who were assembled at the place aforesaid for prevention of rebelion and riots. The Lord Bishop of Carlisle [1] and his daughter were there. By the strictest observation the numbers were twenty-five thousand men,[2] but very few of them had any regular armes. At 11 o'clock in the forenoon of the same day the high sherriff and the two lords received a true account that the Earl of Derwentwater, together with his army, were within 6 miles of Penrith. Vpon the recept of this news the said high sherriff and the said 2 lords, the *posse comitatus* and the malitia fled, leaving most of their armes vpon the said fell. There is no doubt had the men stood their ground the said Earl and his men (as it hath since beene acknowledged by diverse of them) wood have retreated. About 3 aclock in the afternoon on the same day the said Earl, together with his army, in number about one thousand seaven hundred, entred the said towne of Penrith, where they proclaimed their king by

(marginal notes) 2d November 1715 Posse comitatus on Penrith Fell.

Number 25,000.

The Posse comitatus runs away.

2d November 1715. Earl Derwentwater's men, 1700, entred Penrith.

---

[1] William Nicolson, author of the *Historical Library*.

[2] Patten says their number was 14,000, and indicates that it may have been slightly less, though not much.

the name and title of James the 3d of England and Ireland, and 8th of Scotland. In this towne they received what excise was due to the crowne and gave receipts for the same. A small party were sent to Lowther Hall [1] to search for Lord Loynsdale, but not finding him there (for he was gone into Yorkshire), they made bold to take provision for themselves and their horses, such as the Hall aforded. There were only at that time two old woomen in the said Hall who received no bodily

3d November marched to Apleby.

damage. But provision being scarce in the said towne, Penrith, they marched betimes next morning for Apleby. The gentlemen paid their quarters of for what they called for in both these townes, but the commonality paid litle or nothing, neither was there any person that received any bodily damage in either of the said townes. If they found any armes they tooke them without paying the owners for them. Only one man [2] joyned them in their march from Penrith to Apleby. In this towne they made the same proclamation as they had done in the former, and received the excise. The weather at this time for some days before was rainey. They marched out of

5th November marched to Kendall.

this towne betimes on Saturday morning, being the 5th of November, in order for Kendall. In this days march none joyned them (excepting one, Mr. Francis Thornburrow), son of Mr. William Thornburrow of Selfet Hall neare Kendall. His father sent one of his servant men to wait vpon his son because he was in scarlet cloathes, and stile of Captain Thornburrow. [3]

About 12 a'clock of the same day 6 quartermasters came into the towne of Kendall, and about 2 aclock in the afternoone Brigadeer Mackintoss and his men came both a horseback, having both plads on their targets hanging on their backs, either of them a sord by his side, as also either a gun and a case of pistols. The said Brigadeere looked with a grim countenance. He and his man lodged at Alderman Lowrys, a

---

[1] The seat of Viscount Lonsdale.

[2] 'This man stole a horse about one houre before he joyned them, and diserted from them the next day ; and at August Asizes 1716 was found guilty, and executed at Apleby for stealing the said horse.'

[3] 'Mr. Thornburrow was taken at Preston, and brought to Wigan, and hapned to see two other prisoners there bribe the centinel, so they made escape. And one houre after he tould the centinel what he saw. So the centinel let him make his escape in woomen's cloaths.'

private house in Highgate Street in this towne. About one houre after came in the horsemen, and the footmen at the latter end. It rained very hard here this day, and had for several days before, so that the horse and the footmen did not draw their swords, nor shew their collours, neither did any drums beat. Onely six highlands bagpipes played. They marched to the cold-stone or the cross, and read the same proclamation twice over in English, and the reader of it spoke very good English without any mixture of Scotish tongue. I had for about one month lived and was clerke to Mr. Craikenthorp, attorney at Law, and as a spectator I went to heare the proclamation read, which I believe was in print, and began after this manner, vizt., Whereas George Elector of Brunswick has vsurped and taken vpon him the stile of the king of these realms, etc. Another clause in it I tooke particular notice of which was this, vizt.,—Did imedietly after his said fathers decease become our only and lawful leige. At the end of the proclamation they gave a great shout. A quaker who stood next to me not puting of his hat at the end of the said ceremony, a highlander thurst a halbert at him, but it fortunatly went between me and him, so that it did neither of vs any damage. So they dispersed.

In this towne the Earl Derwentwater and his servant lodged at Mr. Fletcher's, the signe of the White Lyon in Strickland Gate, the other lords at Mr. Thomas Pawlandsons who was at that time the mayor of that towne, and kept the signe of Kings Armes in the street above named. Thomas Foster Esquire, then stiled Generall Foster, lodged at Alderman Simpsons, a private house in the said street. They compeled the belman here to go and give notice to the tanners and inkeepers to come and pay what excise was due to the crown or else they that denyed should be plundred by Jack the highlander. They received of the inkeepers and tanners here the summe of eighty pounds and some od shillings, and gave receipts to each person. About six o'clock this night the mayor was taken into custody for not telling where the malitia armes were hid (the said mayor was a leivetenent in the malitia), but next morning Mr. Crosby, the minister of this towne, went to Earl Derwentwater and Thomas Foster and got the mayor discharged out of custody. Madam Belingham (who was godmother to Thomas Foster), and tabled in Mr. Simpsons house, wood not admitt her said godson to see her, and he going vpstairs for that intent, she met him on the stairs, gave him two or three boxes on the eare, and called him a rebel and a popish toole, which he tooke patiently. They made the gunsmiths here work very hard all night and a Sunday morning likewise, for little or no pay. In the house where I lived two Northumberland gentlemen, stiled captains, lodged, who behaved themselves very civily. Some malitious persons had falsely reported that the malitia armes were in the church, and on Sunday morning some of the highlanders broke into the church in expectation of finding armes there. They also went into the vestry in the church. The plate and ornaments belonging to the said church were in the vestry; but finding no armes there returned without taking any of the plate.

In this towne the horse gentlemen paid their quarters, but the foot highlanders paid little or nothing : and about 8 a clock this morning the foot marched out, no drums beating nor collours flying, only the bagpipers playing. Most of the horsemen waited at Foster's quarters. I stood close to Mr. Simpson's doore and the six lords, Brigadeere Mackintosh and Thomas Foster had their hats in their hands. The Brigadeere looked still with a grim countenance, but the lords, Foster, and most of the other horsemen were dishartened and full of sorrow. About 9 aclock the same morning they marched out of the towne (but

6th November. They marched to Kirkby Loynsdale.

not in ranks), a jorniman weaver joyned them here. They marched this day to Kirkby Loynsdale. The horsemen quartered there, and the footmen went to the adjacent vilages and houses. In Kirkby Loynsdale they made the same proclamation, and received what excise was due. Esquire Carus and his two sons Thomas and Christopher, all papists, who lived at Hatton Hall, joyned them at this towne. It was this Carus[1] that first brought them word that the towne of Lancaster had left of making any preparations for a defence; so

7th November. They marched for Lancaster.

they marched for Lancaster next morning, and as they came by

---

[1] 'Carus, the father, dyed at Liverpool, the day before he shood had his tryall. Christopher found guilty at Liverpool, and Thomas pleaded the King's pardon.'

Hornby Castle, whose owner is Francis Chart[er]is, they made bold to call to see if he was there, but not finding him there they took provisions for themselves and their horses. It was about 1 a clock in the afternoon on Monday when they came into Lancaster, where they found that the inhabitants of that towne had taken vp the pavement of the bridge, and the side of the north arch of Lancaster brige. This towne wood have opposed the Earl Derwentwater and his man, and for that purpose the inhabitants intended to fetch the 6 guns belonging to the merchants there, which were at Sunderland in a ship called the Robert, if Sir Henry Houghton, colonel of the malitia, and who was at Preston with his men, had come to Lancaster. They came into this town with swords drawn, drums beating and collours flying, and in their ranks with the bagpipes also playing. They went streight to the market place and made the same proclamation as before. A little after this, one Christopher Hopkins, a stationer, was by the order of Thomas Foster, taken into custody, and put prisoner on the guard, for taking account of the number of them. The folowing esquires who lived some few miles from this towne joyned them here, (viz.), Hodgson of Leighton Hall, John Dalton of Thurnham Hall, John Tyldesley of the Lodge—Butler of Rathliffe [1]—Hilton,[2] who lived near Cartnell. All these attended with their servant men, joyned them as abovesaid (and were stiled captains). Onely two inhabitants of this towne, who were papists, joyned themselves (to witt) Edmund Gartside, a barber, and the other man, whose name I have forgot, was a joyner. These last two men [3] (were stiled quartermasters). In this towne in the evening they received from the inkeepers what excise was due, but it did not amount but to a very little.

Also this night a great consultation was held here whether or no the prisoners in this castle shood be set at liberty, and at first it was vnanimously agreed that the debtors as well as those vpon the Crown side shood all be released from their imprison-

---

[1] Tyldesley acquitted at London; Hodgson, Dalton, and Butler found guilty there.

[2] 'Hilton made his escape at Preston, but now has the benefitt of the King's pardon.'

[3] These 2 made their escape at Preston, but now have the benefitt of the King's pardon.

ment; but vpon a second consideration that onely those vpon
the Crown side shoold be set at liberty, which accordingly was
done. Amongst those released were the colonel and captain of
the Mob of Manchester, whose names I have forgott. These
two men were at Lancaster at the August Assizes before found
guilty of rioting at Manchester, and sentenced to stand in the
pilory at Lancaster (which accordingly they did). Also they
were to continue in Lancaster prison for some years. I was at
Lancaster and saw them stand in the pilory there, which was
vpon a Saturday, being the market day there, about a weeke
after the said assizes, but no person was alowed to fling anything at them. The said colonel and captain joyned and listed
themselves with the said Earl Derwentwater. They still kept
their former titles.[1]

This night 6 highlanders (who were apointed searchers for
armes) by threats compeled Mr. Parkinson, the then mayor of
this towne to goe along with them from house to house to
search for armes. At every house they demanded armes which
if the owner of them did not deliver Jack the highlander was
to plunder him. They got very few small armes here, but those
as they tooke they did not pay for. During their continuance
in this towne the gunsmiths here were well employed in clean-
ing guns and pistols, and received pay for their work. Some
small armes were taken from the minister of this towne, whose
name is James Fenton. The shopkeepers here had little or
no gunpowder; only one whose name is Samuel Satherwaite,
and he thought it properer to bestow a barrell of gunpowder
in the towns well raither than sell it.

Next morning, which was on Tuesday the 8th, by the order
of the said Thomas Foster, a proclamation was issued, in
which a reward of Thirty pounds for any person who could
take Ralph Fairbrother, an inhabitant of this towne, who was
gone post haste with Christopher Hopkins account of the number of the said Earl Derwentwaters men to Generall Carpenter
at Newcastle. Also this day commissioners were apointed to
examine the books belonging to the Custom house here, but

---

[1] 'The colonel and captain made their escape at Preston, but the day after the
colonel was taken, found guilty of high treason at Liverpool, and executed at
Manchester, and his head put vp there.'

found nothing due to the Crown, only a part of a large quantity of brandy (which the Custom house officers had some days before seized, being run from the Isle of Man), the said officers had made vse of a small part of it, and the new comissioners took possession of the remainder, part of which they drank in this towne, and the rest they carryed away in a cart towards Garstang, but they made an end of it before they came to that towne. Also at Lancaster on the said 8th day a detachment were sent to Sunderland to bring vp the said 6 ship guns, which accordingly they did. At 10 aclock this morning, by the order of Mr. Paul, a minister of the Church of England [1] (and who had joyned with the said Earl Derwentwater) a little bell hanging on the east end of Lancaster church was ringed to warne people to come to prayers, and while the said bell was a ringing Mr. Paul tooke the common prayerbooke (which the minister of Lancaster comonly made vse of), and in the prayer for the Queen Mr. Paul razed out the name (Queen Anne) and writ (King James), and [in] the prayer for the royall family he razed out the name of the (Princess Sophia) and writ the (King's Mother). The said words are writ with such a nicety that many takes them to have been printed. Abundance of persons went this day to this church, and the said Mr. Paul read the vsuall prayers, only instead of praying for King George prayed for his new Majesty by the name of King James, and instead of George, prince of Wales, he prayed thus (to bless the king's mother and all the royall family). The minister of Lancaster does not make vse of that book now, but has laid it by in the vestry. This afternoone the gentlemen soldiers dressed and trimmed themselves vp in their best cloathes for to drink a dish of tea with the laydys of this towne. The laydys also here apeared in their best riging, and had their tea tables richly furnished for to entertain their new suitors.

This afternoone a new postmaster was apointed, and when the post came in the new postmaster seized the bag of leters, and amongst them found a bill which the generall postmaster had ordered the postmaster of this town to pay, which was fifty pounds. The new postmaster. . . . This evening a discourse about religion hapned between the minister of this towne

---

[1] Executed for high treason at London.

and two Romish priests. During the continuance of the Earl
Derwentwaters men in this towne no inhabitant received any
bodily damage. The gentleman paid of their commons here,
but very sorrowfull to part with their new loves. The com-
monalty paid little or nothing here.

Next morning being Wednesday 9th both horse and footmen
marcht out of this towne carrying along with them the said
six ship guns and some of the brandy, and their prisoner,
Christopher Hopkins. Him they tooke about two miles and so

9th November.
Foot march to
Garstang, and
horse to
Preston.

dismissed him. The horse came to Preston this night, but the
foot lodged at Garstang and other countrey houses. One Mr.
Monkcaster,[1] a protestant, who was Attorney at law (who lived
in Gartstang) joyned them there. Severall poore papists
joyned them also here. Here also they received what excise
was due. Next day came also the footmen into Preston where
the same proclamation was made here as in former towns.
They also received what excise was due here. Esquire Townley,[2]
a papist, joyned them here, and Mr. Shuttleworth[3] who lived
in Preston, as also did aboundance of Roman Catholicks. The
laydys in this towne, Preston, are so very beautyfull and so
richly atired that the gentlemen soldiers from Wednesday to
Saturday minded nothing but courting and feasting. The day
last mencioned, about one a clock in the afternoon, Generall
Wills with his men came vp to Rible bridge, and from thence
proceeded to Preston. Generall Carpenter and his men came
to that towne on Sunday morning, and on Monday morning the
Earl Derwentwater surrendered the said towne, and he and
all his men that were in that towne made prisoners of war.

It may be expected that I should here give account of the two
generalls Carpenter and Wills proceedings, and of the defence
that the Earl Derwentwater and his men made, as also of the
number that were on both sides killed and wounded. But for
some reasons I shall omitt it, and only take notice that after
the said two generalls men had taken whole possession of the
said towne of Preston, they with force and armes broke open

---

[1] 'Monkaster found guilty of high treason at Liverpool, and executed at
Preston.'

[2] 'He was tryed at London and found not guilty.'

[3] 'Mr. Shutleworth executed at Preston, and his head put vp there.'

doers and locks of chambers and clossetts, and the moneys, plate, goods, and chatles of most of the inhabitants of that towne (who were and still are good subjects to his Majestie's King Georges government), contrary to the will of the owners of the said goods, felonyously did steal, take, and carry away contrary to his said Majestie's peace, crowne, and dignity, and also contrary to the laws of the nation in that case made and provided.—I am, Sir, Your humble servant,

PETER CLARKE.

(Postscript in same handwriting.)

Upon Saturday the 12th November 1715, about 11 a clock in the forenoone, the Earl Derwentwater ordered 300 horsemen to go to Rible bridge to oppose Generall Wills passage over it. But about one houre after Generall Wills and his men came into Walton in Ledale, neare vnto the said Rible bridge, the said Earl Derwentwaters men retired into Preston, and there they made a trensh and a baracade over against the Church in Church gate Preston, and there placed two of the ship guns charged with small bullets; and at the out ends of this towne they made trences. About 2 a clock this afternoone 200 of Generall Wills men entred the Churchgate Street, and the Highlanders firing out of the cellers and windows, in 10 minuits time kiled 120 of them. The Highlanders also fired the said 2 ship guns, but the bullets flew vpon the houses, so that no execution was done thereby. A little time after this a party was sent to burne the houses and barnes where the Highlanders wer at the entrance of the said Church gate Street, and accordingly severall houses and barnes were burnt, and so forced the Highlanders to move vp further into this towne. At this time the wind was north, which if it had been south, the judicious are of opinion that most of this towne would have been burnt. About 4 a clock the same day 300 men were commanded to enter the back Street called the back Ween in Preston, and accordingly they made an attempt. But the Highlanders placing themselves vnder gardens, walls, hedges, and dickes kiled the captain and about 140 of his men. Night now aproching, Generall Wills men camped round this towne, and also burnt severall houses and barnes att the north end of it.   Also this night severall of the Earl Derwentwaters men made their escape out of this towne.   Also about 10 a clock next morning Generall Carpenter and his men came vp and camped round this towne, but did not burne neither house or barnes.   Some few men on both sides were kiled this forenoone ; but in the afternoone a cessiation of armes were agreed on by both sides, and next morning the Earl Derwentwater and his men surrendered, and were made prisoners of war.   By the strictest observacion of the number of Earl Derwentwaters men that were there kiled were 18 or 19, and of Generalls Carpenter and Wills men two hundred and seaventy.

II.

EIGHT LETTERS by WILLIAM NICOLSON, D.D., Bishop of Carlisle, to SIR WILLIAM DAWES, Archbishop of York, 1716.

CARLISLE, December the 8th, 1716.

YESTERDAY the judges open'd their commission here, three of them (and about eight or ten of the neighbouring Justices of the Peace who were join'd with them), being present in court.

Baron Price,[1] being seiz'd with a fit of the gout, kept his chamber. Mr. Justice Tracy[2] gave a short, but very handsome charge, wherein he set forth the contents of the Act of Parliament that supported the tryals of the prisoners brought hither from Edinburgh, with the legality and reasonableness whereof all the judges of England were so well satisfy'd, that every one of them had (in their turns) sat on the tryals of Scotchmen (and their conviction) in Middlesex, Surrey, etc. He observed that the government had now pitch'd on Carlisle, as being the nearest to the friends of those that were to be arraign'd ; so that no just complaint could be made of their witnesses being at a great distance, etc. There was also, he said, a special regard had to the loyalty of this county ; where, if anywhere, honest juries might be hoped for on this occasion.

Thus far we have pretty well answer'd those kind hopes. Three bills were immediately prefer'd against twelve of the prisoners ; and *billa vera* found against eleven of them. The twelfth was one Mr. Maul, chamberlaine (or steward) to the

---

[1] Sir Robert Price, Baron of the Exchequer, afterwards a justice of the Common Pleas.

[2] Sir Robert Tracy, justice of the Common Pleas.

Earl of Panmure,[1] against whom no peremptory, but a little hearsay evidence (which amounted to nothing), was produced ; and indeed nothing less than *ignoramus* seem'd to be expected by the manager for the king, so that the putting the matter on such an experiment looks mystical.

Both judges and sollicitor-general[2] gives fair encouragement to plead guilty, and I hope a great many will venture upon what they understand to be a parole of honour in the government. The only scruple is, that conviction forfeits their estates; and some of them, unwilling to live without their lairdships, seem resolved (on that score) to run the risque of neck and all. What they have heard of the hanging of three or four at Preston (this last summer), after they had been thus prevail'd with to condemn themselves, sticks in the gizzards of several.

Neither of our temporal lords in the commission (Earl of Carlile[3] and Lord Lonsdale[4]) are in the country. The former has indeed liv'd long in Yorkshire; but his friends here hop'd that (on this occasion) his lordship would have countenanc'd them with his presence. The later left us just as the judges were upon the confines of the county.

One of the knights of our shire (Mr. James Lowther) was summon'd as fore-man of the grand jury, and 'twas the general expectation that he would greedily have accepted the office; but, instead of that, he insisted on his privilege of parliament, and threaten'd the sherif with a complaint above, if he should dare to return him in court. Hereupon he was struck out of the list, and tho' he's in the commissions with the judges, keeps at home. These things bring (or increase) a load on those that are present.

The court is just now (at eleven) going to arraign those against whom bills are found; and 'tis hop'd that most of them will plead guilty. More of this by the next.

The weather is terribly cold. A great snow has kept back our last night's post, not yet come in.

---

[1] James, fourth Earl, who was taken prisoner at the battle of Sheriffmuir, but succeeded in escaping to France.

[2] Sir John Fortescue Aland, afterwards Lord Fortescue.

[3] Charles Howard, third Earl of Carlisle.

[4] Henry Lowther, third Viscount Lonsdale.

CARLISLE, December 10th, 1716.

My good Lord,—I am going home this morning, upon promise to return on Saturday, when the tryals of our prisoners first begin. The grand jury goes on without any rub, finding indictments against a round dozen ev'ry day. We doubt whether the petit jurors will equally answer expectation, since the sherif (tho' there was no manner of occasion for it) has blended so many dissenters with the church-men, as will endanger an untoward fermentation.

Last Saturday night on of the clergy-men in town, whom I had appointed to read prayers at the Castle, acquainted me that some of the prisoners (against whom bills of indictment were found) desir'd to receive the sacrament yesterday, which he demurr'd to 'til he had my orders in the matter. I wish'd him to return to them forthwith, and to make those demands which were requisite for their satisfying him of the state of their faith, and withall to let them know (tho' I was far from ensnaring any of them into a needless hazard of their lives or fortunes, yet) I hop'd that, as they had join'd in prayer for King George, as many of them as were truely conscious of their guilt, would sincerely repent of their rebellion against him ; I wish'd him also to hint, that confession would be the most likely way of obtaining mercy both from God and the king.

He brought me thanks from them all, and assurances from some (who have no estate to forfeit), that they will throw themselves entirely upon his majesty's mercy, by pleading guilty. The landed lairds hop'd that I would give them leave to endeavour their exculpation (as they call'd it), to preserve a livelyhood to themselves and families ; protesting that, if the government seiz'd all they had, they'd as soon be hang'd as be starv'd. What reply can one make to these miserable creatures ?

Last night I was visited by the two sollicitors-general (of England and Scotland) and Mr. Carter,[1] the king's counsel.

---

[1] Sir Lawrence Carter, M.P. for Leicester and Beeralston between 1698 and 1715. He became Solicitor-General to the Prince of Wales in 1717, King's Sergeant in 1724, and was knighted, and in 1726 succeeded Baron Price as a Judge in Exchequer. He died at Leicester, unmarried, in 1745.

Whilst they were with me, Mr. Kettleby (counsel for the prisoners) brought me compliments from a friend in your neighbourhood.

By some hints that were given amongst these combatants on both sides, I guess we shall have a plea against the jurisdiction of the court, or rather a protestation against the tenour of their commission, as violating the fundamental articles of the Treaty of Union. I never yet heard of a court that fail'd in asserting its own jurisdiction; and 'twould be an extraordinary sight to have four wise men return hence with a report, that (having open'd their bag *a de secretis* at Carlisle), they found nothing but a pig in the poke.

I am not able to write one word more, if indeed I could tell what. My fingers are very much numm'd. Let me only request your communicating the inclos'd list to my Lord of Canterbury,[1] with the humble duty of your lordship's entirely affectionate brother,

W. CARLIOL.

P.S.—I have, since the writing of this, receiv'd your letter. Whether our Bishop of Bangor will accept of a western translation, he can best tell; tho' (some say) he has lately written a book in Cornish, no English-man being able to understand it.

DECEMBER 13TH, 1716.

MY VERY GOOD LORD,—I gave your grace a sort of a journal of the two first day's work of our Lords of Session at Carlisle; and I hop'd to have been as full handed every post. But the giving of copies of the several indictments to the parties concern'd a week before their respective tryals obliges the judges to direct the prosecutions to be brought on more slowly than they were at the beginning. This expedient is also necessary for the keeping the jurors themselves in daily employment. So that the King's sollicitors fee'd these men with bills as our farmer's fodder their cattle this hard weather, in small quantities, that the stock of provisions may last the longer.

Yesterday they brought in ignoramus on a bill against Mr. Burnet; a kinsman of the late Bishop of Sarum's, and one

---

[1] William Wake, formerly Bishop of Lincoln.

that some time sojourn'd in his family. This unhappy man (as thousands more) was swept away with the high tides of rebellion in his neighbourhood; and surrender'd himself at the first opportunity to some of the King's officers.

One of these was produced as evidence against him. But he could only say that this gentleman was said to be one of those that fell into the hands of a party under his command ; tho' he could not positively swear that he was so ; nor did he remember whether he was taken, or came in voluntarily. Whether the managers for the King will desire that this gentleman may continue a while longer in custody (as Mr. Maul, in the same condition) 'til more prompt witnesses can be had, or he'l shortly be discharg'd, I can't tell. His country-men generally give him a fair character.

Others daily plead guilty; begging in order thereunto to be forthwith arraign'd. Two of these were told by the Chief Baron Smith[1] (with the austerity of a Roman Senator) that —— They who threw themselves upon the Kings mercy would probably find mercy ; and that they that insisted on justice would as probably have justice for their lot. Notwithstanding all which caution, 'tis yet confidently believ'd, that the counsel for the prisoners will (on Saturday next) offer a plea against the jurisdiction, or legal establishment of the court, which may happen to provoke. Another crotchet is talk'd of, —— The challenging the arraies of all our juries (Grand and Petit) as return'd by an improper officer, because, forsooth, our present sherif is collector of the King's customs at Whitehaven. What law there is for support of such a plea I know not. That the same person may be employ'd in several trusts is certainly agreeable to ancient and modern practice in his Majesties court of St. James's. And I see no reason why the like prerogative should not hold good for pluralities of the same nature in the country.

I design (God willing) to attend the debates of that day ; and your Grace shall have the result of them. It will be im-practicable, I doubt, to send it by that day's post ; or perhaps anything else.

We have here the deepest snow, (most of it fallen the last

---

[1] John Smith, Chief Baron of Exchequer in Scotland.

night) that has been seen in many years. This, considering
the slender produce of hay, which the last summer afforded
us, will make it difficult to provide for that great additional
number of horses, which are continually pouring in from all
corners of the island. If we can stand this shock, nothing
will occasion despair in your Grace's most obedient and
oblig'd servant,

W. CARLIOL.

CARLISLE, DECEMBER 15TH, 1716.

THE Scotch advocates, who are assign'd counsel for the
prisoners, have all along threatned the court with (what they
call a declinatour) a plea of demurrer to the jurisdiction.
But 'tis hop'd that this morning, the first (and only) opportunity they have of putting such a design in execution, the
matter will be dropp'd. To this purpose the judges adjourn'd
from Thursday to this day; and both that evening and
yesterday conferences have been had betwixt the King's
sollicitors and them. What is ageed on (if anything) I have
not yet learn'd; but may perhaps learn before the post goes
out, early enough to give an account in the end of this
paper.

Amongst the gentlemen that have pleaded guilty, there's
one Mr. Murray (of Auchterlase, whose brother attempted to
corrupt the guard), much commended for a modest speech at
the bar; which concluded with words to this purpose, ——
That tho' he had reason enough to believe that a jury might
acquit him, he had rather lived under the comfort of the
King's mercy than the load of a guilty conscience.

Sir Thomas Calder[1] (a young baronet who has given in the
same plea) declar'd that he never had any aversion to the
present Government, but being a vassal to the Marquis of
Huntley, he thought himself oblig'd to follow the fortunes of
his lands-lord; of which he now most heartily repents; and
threw himself entirely at the feet of his liege sovereign King
George.

The other of chief note are Colonel Urquart,[2] and Mr. Carnegie

---

[1] Second baronet of Muirtoune, in Morayshire.

[2] Probably Alexander Urquhart of Newhall.

of Finhaven,[1] who are both nearly related to the D. of Montrose, by whose good advice 'tis suppos'd they came thus early into these hopeful measures.

On Thursday the Grand Jury brought in a third *ignoramus* for want of sufficient evidence on a bill against one Mr. Spance. And 'tis said, that not only in this, and in that on Mr. Burnet's bill, but in most of their other verdicts, they have been entirely unanimous. I am sure they have thus far acted to the satisfaction of the judges. I heartily wish the Petit Juries may deserve the like approbation; and I hope they will. However, 'tis a comfort to see so many laying hold of (their only anchor of hope) the King's mercy, and the appearance there is of others reaching at it.

The declinatour is declin'd. The prisoners thus far strive who shall be foremost in pleading guilty. Eleven have this day put in that plea, and no appearance yet of any one man's standing his tryal, saving one Mr. M'Kenzie of Frazerdale, whose story (as it has been given to me) is too long to report. So that, upon the whole, our judges are like to have much shorter work than they expected.

John Ross (the Bishop of Edinburgh's son) came this moment to the Bar; and desir'd a present arraignment, pleaded guilty, and made so handsome an application to the court, that his case is sure of being favourably represented.

Rose, December 17, 1716.

My very good Lord,—My Saturday's postscript was written in such haste that I had not time to acquaint your Grace that the honour of your letter came to my hand when I was with Mr. Justice Tracy, who had acquainted me with a like application in favour of the Bishop of Edinburgh's son, made

---

[1] James Carnegie of Finhaven, a grandson of David, second Earl of Northesk. He was at the battle of Sheriffmuir; and in one of the ballads is represented as showing as much earnestness in flight as the rest—

' Save the laird o' Finhaven, who swore to be even
Wi' any general or peer o' them a', man.

In 1728 he was tried for killing the Earl of Strathmore, at Forfar, by a sword-thrust in a drunken bout. But as the blow had been intended for another companion who had grossly insulted him, the earl's death was considered accidental, and he was acquitted.

to himself by the Earl of Caernarvon.[1] Two such advocates were soon agreed to be worth a whole threeve of them from the North ; and thereupon I had leave to send for the young fellow forthwith to the Bar; where he presently appeared, desired to be immediately arraing'd, and (that being granted) pleaded guilty. This he did in so becoming a manner, and so good an appearance of a true penitent heart, that the judge promised to represent his case favourably to his Majesty, whose mercy he confidently relies on. I had never seen the young man's face before, but was not a little pleased with his modest behaviour.

The Scottish Counsel are very impatient for want of an opportunity to open their portmantcaus, wherein they are said to have brought many and large volumes of records, for the ascertaining of the legal privileges and immunities of the ancient kingdom. Several of them open very loud on this occasion. But the most obstreperous is reported to be one Mr. Graham,[2] a person of great learning and eminence. He is the King's Judge of the Admiralty in Edinburgh, and (in the warmth of his zeal) has procured leave to be of counsel for the prisoners, on purpose to dispute this point, which he declares he'l maintain to the hazard of his very life, as well as his fortunes. The judges seem to hope that they shall be able to ward off this argument. And indeed the Sollicitor-General and the rest of our English counsel, on the Crown side, appear as loath to engage in it.

Mr. Mackenzie of Frazerdale[3] (against whom an indictment was found by the Grand Jury on Saturday last) seems to be the likeliest person to bring on the debate. This gentleman's case has been so variously represented that (without a formal tryal) no body can tell what to make of it. Some stoutly affirm, as himself does, that he never bore arms in the Pre-

---

[1] James Brydges, afterwards Duke of Chandos.

[2] James Graham, afterwards Dean of the Faculty of Advocates. He was ancestor of the family of Graham of Airth Castle in Stirlingshire.

[3] Formerly Alexander Mackenzie of Prestonhall. He married, in 1702, the heiress of Lovat, and assumed the name of Fraser, changing Lovat into Fraserdale, of which he had the liferent. This, however, he lost on his attainder for his part in the rebellion. He and his son Hugh had a long and keen contest with the famous Simon Fraser, Lord Lovat, as to the title of Lovat.

tender's camp, that he was carried prisoner into Perth, and
thence made his escape before the battle of Dumblain. Others
say that (upon a family disgust) he did freakishly join the
rebels at first ; but saw his error pretty early, and stole off to
the Duke of Athol. His Grace strongly avows his just claim
to remission, or rather an acquittal, and has sent Lord James,
now Lord Tullibardin,[1] to sollicit his cause. On the other
hand, Lord Lovat has seiz'd the life rent of his estate, and will
probably be desirous to continue in possession.

I have inclos'd a list of all that had bills found against them
by the Grand Jury, when I came away on Saturday in the
evening ; to which I believe I may add Brigadier Campel, a
bill being prefer'd against him that day. This unfortunate
man was in no engagement, and had not been four days in
Scotland, when he was taken in one of the Western Islands.
He has been in foreign service (under the Czar, the Venetians,
etc.) from his youth ; and I dare parole for him, if the Government sends him back to the Adriatick Coast, he'l never peti-
tion for another return into his native country.—I am, your
Grace's most obedient servant,   W. CARLIOL.

Rose, December 20th, 1716.

MY VERY GOOD LORD,—By the last post I told your Grace
that if the Scotch Advocates did produce their declinatour, I
had hopes of hearing what they had to offer on that head. It
has happen'd otherwise. For, upon Monday last, they sur-
priz'd the Court (with their arguments) in favour of one Mr.
William Hay, whose name your Grace will find in the list of
the indicted. I am promis'd a copy of their pleadings in form.
Till that comes, be pleas'd to take such an account of 'em as I
have had from some present.

1st. They began with protestations that on the Treaty of
Union the realm of Scotland was a right ancient and inde-
pendant kingdom, and that accordingly its Commissioners
treated (on the square and level) with those of England.
That the stipulations therein were mutual and inviolable, as
(by the law of nations) they ought to be. In the course of
this preliminary article they did great honour to the Bishop

---

[1] Afterwards second Duke of Athole.

of Carlisle, in frequently citing his Preface to the *Border Laws*, etc.

2. They observed that in their Justiciary Courts, which were established by the foresaid Treaty, the subjects of Scotland were indulg'd a list of the witnesses that were to be produc'd against them, as well as several other privileges of value, which they are here debar'd of.

3. By their *Habeas Corpus Act*, no Scotch man could be carry'd out of that kingdom without his own consent, which was to be solemnly recorded.

4. That the Act of Parliament for speedy tryals, etc. (whereon the jurisdiction of the present Court is found), was never intended to reach North Britain. This they thought plainly appear'd from its preamble, wherein the chief reason for its being enacted is said to arise from its being inconvenient to the publick justice of the nation *that the judges should remain so long in the said counties as will be necessary for the trying of the said offenders,* whereas, said they, it had been much more convenient for the publick justice of the Scottish nation (as well as for the judges themselves) that these gentlemen should have been try'd at Edinburgh rather than at Carlisle.

5. This Act pretends not to direct the tryal of any persons whatever, saving only such as shall be *apprehended and committed to prison on or before the 23rd of January* 1716. Now, according to the calculation of the *Kirk of Scotland* (which no man will deny stands most firmly ratify'd by the Act of Union), that day was over before any of the prisoners were either committed or apprehended, and indeed before the Act itself was in being.

These were the objections which were offerd. The *third* is said to have weighed most with one of the judges. And yet (with great submission) it appears to me to be a very light one, if we consider that their Act of Habeas Corpus pass'd in 1701 ; and therefore (*quoad hoc*) must be repeal'd by the 23rd Article of Union.

The *fourth*, in my poor opinion, is all that is worth the considering ; especially since (which was observ'd by the counsel) no mention is made of stewartries, but only of counties and shires. But, since the letter of the law is capable of another construction, and our judges have already constru'd it otherwise, both in Middlesex and Surrey, it could not reasonably be hop'd that this could stagger them now.

Neither they, nor their Sollicitor General thought fit to make any reply; but the prisoner was allow'd to consider, whether he'd insist on his demurrer 'til the morning: when he withdrew it, and pleaded guilty.

I do not think that any one of them will stand a tryal. They seem unanimously to long and pray for the King's happy return; hoping that he will thereupon spread his royal mantle of mercy over them all. I cannot help saying Amen to the whole prayer.

Our judges, under the rose, hope to finish their whole work this week; or at least before Christmas Day, and think of returning southward about this day sennight, or Wednesday next. They, and Lord James Murray, etc., have threatned to dine with me to day. But, perhaps, the change of the weather (tho' they have nothing to do at Carlisle before to morrow) may possibly prevent their coming. However, a fair competency of powder'd beef and cabbage is provided for them by your Grace's most obedient servant,

W. CARLIOL.

Rose, December 22nd, 1716.

MY VERY GOOD LORD,—After so long a tale as your Grace had from me by the last post, no great matters will be expected by this. For the diversion of the counsel there was yesterday another plea argu'd. Mr. Trullock, by his advocates, challeng'd the array of the Petit Jury, as return'd by an incompetent officer. The substance of the plea was:—The Sherif is a servant (a collector of customs) under his Majesty; and therefore incapable of returning a jury in any cause wherein the King is plaintif. The Statute of Lincoln (9 Ed. 2) and other laws were quoted. The King's counsel answer'd amongst other arguments, that the Sherif of a county was the most proper collector of all the King's revenues within his bayliwick; and that, therefore, this was far from being a reasonable and legal objection. They also observed, that the

Sherifs employment (as customes) was held by deputation
from the commissioners, and not immediately from the King;
that it was an insignification trifle, of £10 salary, etc.

In short, the court over-rul'd the plea; and culprit was
appointed to abide his tryal (if he thought fit, as 'tis believ'd
he will not) on Wednesday next. No Pettit Jury yet em-
panell'd.

For want of matter from Oyer and Terminer, give me leave
(my good Lord) to open my heart, much oppress'd, to your
Grace on another subject. I have this week, at a very improper season, gotten my brother of B——s book [1] in answer to
the pleaders of schism, etc. I am, to morrow, by God's leave,
to hold an ordination; And there are several passages in this
book that exceedingly perplex me. I have no quarrel with
the man about his justifying of the deprivation of bishops;
nor shall I insist on his calling the *succession of prelates from
the apostolical times* a trifle. But — shall our people be
taught that they are not to expect any of *God's graces, bene-
dictions, or absolutions from any hands but his own?* Must I
believe that the commission given by our Saviour, *Whosoever
sins* etc., refer'd to *something extraordinary and supernatural
in the Apostles for the propagation of the Gospel only at the
first; and not to anything in the ordinary settl'd condition of
the Church.* How then shall I dare to use the same form of
words, in the *ordaining of an ordinary presbyter?*

Again, must I (my Lord) agree that the human engines (as
he calls 'em) of bennidictions, absolutions and excommunica-
tions *have nothing to do with the favour or anger of God?*

Nothing of this kind is allow'd by him to *be authoritative.*
I do therefore beg of your Grace to let me know what sort of
authority it was that your predecessor [2] (at my consecration)
committed to me, with a charge that I should use it not to
destruction but to salvation; and what was that *Spirit of
Power* that was then given me?

The reading of this book, my Lord, has more (a thousand

---

[1] Probably Benjamin Hoadley, Bishop of Bangor, whose writings on the
Church question gave rise to much debate, especially to what is known as the
Bangorian Controversy in the following year.

[2] Archbishop John Sharp.

times) disquieted my thoughts than all the clutter we have
had with our prisoners. It may be (and I pray God it may
be) that I do not fathom the author's meaning;—That all he
says is reconcileable to the doctrine of our establish'd Church ;
and that the fault of his not being understood, is wholy my
own. I do earnestly, once more, wish this may be the true
state of the case ; And am ever, my good Lord, your Grace's
most obedient Servant,

                                            W. CARLIOL.

                        ROSE, December 24th, 1716.

MY VERY GOOD LORD,—Since the last post nothing has come
from Carlisle worth the reporting, save what happen'd on
Saturday, too late for me to mention. The judges were
pleas'd to dismiss the Grand Jury, with very obliging acknow-
ledgements of the faithful discharge of their trust, so that no
more of the prisoners are like to have any bills prefer'd against
them, tho' near thirty are as yet untouched.

Two gentlemen of the name of Stuart were the last against
whom any bill was found, and Mr. Sollicitor acquainted the
Court, that (tho' these were hurried hither with their com-
panions yet) they were so far from bringing any guilt along
with them, that he should think himself oblig'd to sue for a
recompence from the Government for their good services.
They are said to have been sent out by the Duke of Athol to
hinder several from joyning in the rebellion ; and to have
done it effectually ; but were not, it seems, in a condition to
set their matters in a fair light 'til they were brought as far
south as Carlisle. Here we live in a clear air.

                        December 27th.

MY LORD,—The foregoing page was just finished on Monday last, when I was surpris'd with a visit from the two
Sollicitors General (of England and Scotland) and all the
King's counsel ; who having that day at their own disposal,
very kindly disposed it in dining with me. At their return
in the evening they found that Brigadier Campbel (whom
they thought the most likely person to stand his tryal) had
slipp'd thro' the gaolers fingers, and was gone off. I was

much encourag'd to hope that this Gentleman would plead
guilty. His flight, and the manner of it, is ye a mystery;
but his keeper is shrewdly suspected to have been privy to the
plot.

All the four judges have had copies of Master Douglas's
case, and are inclineable enough to give credit to its contents.
The man's misfortune was great in his unmannerly receipt of
the transcript of his indictment at the Bar; which was taken
to be the effect of a peculiar stubborness, and his being
harden'd in his iniquity. But they are, I believe, convinced
that the awkwardness of his mien (on that occasion) did not
proceed from any want of a proper sense of his condition. I
cannot well apprehend that above a Couple will be executed.

To shew your Grace how sedulous our northern Jacobites
are to keep up their sinking cause in spight of all justice and
gibbetts, I have inclosed another of the Edinburgh libels that
are scatter'd amongst our people, to move their hearts to
tender compassions, and traiterous conspiracies.

Your Grace is so sure of my obeying your summons, whenever
my attendance is necessary, that I do humbly hope that you
will grant me as long a dispensation for staying at home as
can conveniently, at least, be afforded. I am far from being in
right keeping for an immediate journey with the judges. I
want to be recruited in some particulars wherein they abound.
'Tis very probable they may leave us to-morrow, for I am just
now told that their Petit Jury (by Judge Tracy's special
direction) brought in the only person they have to try not
guilty. I expect the particulars of this report every minute;
and (if they are worth it) they'l be dispatch'd to my Lord of
Lincoln by your Grace's ever obedient servant,

W. CARLIOL.

III.

LEAVES from the diary of John Campbell, an Edinburgh Banker in 1745.

Saturday, 14 September 1745.

On news of the Highland army's approach, all the effects of the Bank were packt up, and partly transported to the Castle this night, per memorandum apart.

Sunday, 15th.

The rest of the Bank effects transported to the Castle.

Monday, 16th September.

Received a letter from Lord Justice Clerk[1] desiring me to let him have £100. A Highland gentleman of Earl Loudoun's regiment deliverd me this letter in the Castle of Edinburgh, on which I came down for my keys, met the Justice Clerk on the street, desired me to give the money to his Lady with whom he was to leave bank notes or draft on his cash account for the value; went back to the Castle, took the money in half guineas out of my balance chest there, returnd to Edinburgh, deliverd the £100 to Lady Milnton[2] in her own house but got no value, nor have I seen the Justice Clerk since. Highland army near Edinburgh per Courant. I dined with Coulterallars.[3] Saw the Dragoons run off along the north side of Edinburgh.[4] The town in a consternation all day. Volunteers arms deliverd in to the Castle on allarm of the fire-

---

[1] Andrew Fletcher of Milton.
[2] Elizabeth Kinloch (of Gilmerton), his wife.
[3] Mr. Robert Menzies of Coulterallers, Writer to the Signet.
[4] This was the incident known as the Canter of Coltbridge.

bell in the evening. Deputation of the Magistracy sent out to Bellsmilns to capitulate with the Prince as to the surrender of the town, without effect.

Tuesday, 17 September.
Edinburgh taken by the Highland army; 1200 Men sent in early in the morning. Numbers of Highlanders crowd in to town all the day long. Sundry proclamations over the Cross. Prince enters Holyroodhouse. His army encamps in the King's park.

Wednesday, 18th September.
Mercury published an account of taking of Edinburgh and proceedings of the army for some days preceeding.

Thursday, 19 September.
Highland army decamped from Dudingston late at night.

Friday, 20th September.
Highland army march towards Tranent and ly on their arms all night thereabouts. General Cope gets in to a fastness [1] below to the north of them towards the sea.

Saturday, 21 September.
Battle of Gladsmuir or Tranent fought wherin the Highlanders routed General Cope.

| Notified per Express* *Jock | { | to Lord Monzie [2] Auchalader [3] Lord Glenorchy [4] |
| D⁰· per post to | { | Lady Glenorchy [5] Mr Mathias |

Had a letter from G. Innes calling me up to the Castle about sundrys and went, and gave out some money out of my balance per memorandum left in the chest.

---

[1] Preston Tower.
[2] Patrick Campbell of Monzie, a lord of Session.
[3] John Campbell of Auchalader.
[4] John Campbell, afterwards third Earl of Breadalbane.
[5] Arabella Pershall, his Countess.

Sunday, 22d September.

No sermon in the Churches.

Monday, 23 September.

Mercury published giving an account of the battle and Journal of the Army from 27th August to this date. It likewise contains serious reflections theron. Directors proposd to burn notes in the Castle and sent me there to obtain access for them.

Tuesday, 24.

Courant published an imperfect account of the battle. A message from G. I.[1] signifying the directors would have access to the Castle when they pleased, but they delay'd cancelling the notes for some time.

Wednesday, 25 September.

Received £200 Silver from A. Brown's son. Earl B.[2] drew on me to D[u] Dun[can] Cam[pbell] for a guinea which I paid him per receipt. Had a message from G. I. for money and went up to the Castle, saw him and his wife and did some business there. Mercury published containing 3 sundry proclamations by the Prince.

Thursday, 26 September 1745.

I was calld upon by Mr. J. Philp to go to the Castle. Went with him. Saw General Guest. Gave General Guest 50lb. in half guineas out of my balance on Lord Justice Clerks draught which I lodg'd in chest in the Castle. Chang'd £5 note to Mr. David Lyon in the Castle and gave him gold for same out of my balance having lodg'd that note in the chest. On my return from the Castle din'd at home *solus*. Called a meeting of directors at 3 oclock and Messrs. Hamilton, Shairp and Philp met, and were of opinion they could not without a quorum order out the money wanted by G. I. and read and approvd of a letter I wrote to him to that effect. Got a letter from St. Germains[3] by his servant telling of his bad usage by the Highlanders. In consequence of which I wrote to Mr. J.

---

[1] George Innes.   [2] Earl of Breadalbane.
[3] St. Germains was a seat of the Seton family in East Lothian.

Murray at Earl Breadalbane's to get a protection and pass.
To call at Mr. J. Murray tomorrow's morning about St. Germain's protection and pass.

Friday, 27th.

Went to the Abbey to see Earl Breadalbane who told me
the Prince was visiting him last night. Saw Mr. J. Murray
who told me he would send up the protection for St Germans
and pass, as soon as obtaind. Saw Mr. Philp about cash for
G. I. but he did not incline to grant warrant. Call'd to see if
Mr. Coutts was come home to try if he would concurr but was
not. Call'd at the Chancery and got up Earl Breadalbanes
patent of honour which lay there to be recorded in terms of the
Interlocutor of the Lords of Session, it having been neglected
at passing the same in 1681. But delay'd taking out the
Extract, and in case I was not to take it out at all, am to pay
for the writing. Told Mr. Philp that Provost Coutts was not
come to town. Dined at home, J. C., Supervisor, with me.
Got a letter from Auchalader desiring to get him a suit of
cloaths which I bespoke at James Stirlings. Mercury published with a proclamation about the Banks, and rectifying
some articles formerly published as to the battle, also publish-
ing the Act of Regency and Manifesto. Saw Mr. Trotter
who told me he has Provost Coutt's Bank-key. Got a protection for the estate, houses and effects of St. Germain's and
allowance for passing and repassing about his lawfull affairs,
and gave Mr. Murrays servant 2s. 6d. Bespoke a frize coat
for my self at James Stirlings, and orderd Niccol to make it.

Saturday, 28 September.

Dispatched St. Germain's servant home with the protection.
Sent to Mr. Trotter for Provost Coutts Bank-key which I got
seald. Advis'd Messrs. Hamilton and Philp that I had got the
key, and they have appointed ½ past ten to go to the Castle to
settle with G. Innes. I sent to the accomptant and tellers to
attend. We all went up to the Castle gate, but could not get
access. G. I. was insulted by the officer of the Guard. Wrote
to Auchalader telling I had bespoke his cloths and sent him
last Mercury by the man who came in with the clerk's son, and

sent him at the same time a pound Bohea tea at 9 shillings
from James Stirlings. Took leave of Captain M'Nab, he being
to sett out by 6 next morning to Perth with the rest of the
officers who are prisoners. Took leave of Ensign Allan Campbell, prisoner.

Sunday, 29 September.

No sermon in churches. Din'd at home, D. B.[1] with me.
Mr. James Veitch calld upon us and went together to John's
Coffee house. In the evening G. Innes calld upon me, he
having come down from the Castle the night before.

Monday, 30 September.

Had a Message from E. B. to dine with him, but can't
comply because of the consternation the town is in, the Castle
having threatned to fire if the Highland guard at the Weigh-
house was not removd.   Got home 6 new shirts and paid
Margaret Jack for cambrick and making £1. 10. therof £1.
formerly lodg'd with Betty for buying the cambrick.   Inhabitants met in new Church to consult on a letter they had
received from General Guest threatning that unless the communication between the City and Castle was opened they
would fire upon the City.   Deputies therupon sent from the
City of Edinburgh to the Prince with General Guests letter ;
to which the Prince gave an answer which is now printed.
On this answer hostilities from the Castle suspended for 6
days.   Numbers of the inhabitants movd their families and
effects out of town all this day.   The City being somewhat
calm'd, about 1 oClock I went down to the Abbey where all
was quiet, dined with E. B. and Mr. Murray.   Return'd at 3
in a chair, came home.   Went to the Coffee house, there
staid till the evening that I came home for all the night.   Sent
messages to Lord Monzie and Lord Tinwalds Servants to
pacify them as to their fears and to several other families of
my acquaintance.

Tuesday, 1 October 1745.

Had a verbal message from Provost Coutts now at Allan-
bank, per his friend, Mr. Coutts, about Bank affairs.   Between

---

[1] David Baillie.

6 and 7 oclock at night a protest was then taken against me,
as Cashier of the Royal Bank, by John Murray of Broughton
Esq. as Secretary to the Prince, for payment of £857 Royal
Bank Notes (which he exhibited), in the current coin of the
kingdom, and on failyure therof within 48 hours, that the
estates and effects of the directors and managers should be
distress'd for the same. I answer'd that by reason of the com-
motion in the countrey, the effects of the Bank were lately
carried up to the Castle, for the security of all concern'd, for
as the directors acted, in a manner, as factors for their constituents, the proprietors, it was judg'd reasonable, and what
every body in their circumstances had done, to secure the
effects of the Company, that none might be sufferers in the
issue : and matters were in that situation at present that there
was no access to the Castle at any rate, for that Mr. Jo.
Hamilton and Mr. John Philp, two of the directors, had
essayed to get in on Saturday last with the accomptant and
tellers and myself in order to do business, but that access was
refused, tho' they continued at the gate for about an hour.
Duply'd by Mr. Murray that he would in name of the Prince
grant a pass and protection *for going to the gate,* and that he
hoped the Governor would give admittance. But whether he
did or not, if the payment was not made, the order should be
put in execution, after clapse of the time limited ; and thereupon took instruments in the hands of William M'Kewan,
notary publick, in presence of Mr. Peter Smith, brother to
deceast David Smith of Methven, and   Purves, Writer
to the Signet ; and thereafter a schedule of the protest was
sent to me by Mr. M'Kewan the notar, but not sign'd. Immediately on Mr. Murray's taking the above protest I waited
upon Mr. Jo. Hamilton and Mr. Philp, the only two directors
in town, at Mrs. Clerks, vintner, there shewed them the
schedule, and what I have before here marked down, and after
reasoning theron agreed to try to get into the Castle to morrow,
and orderd Mr. Shairp, the only other director about the town,
to be summond for that purpose, to meet with them at my
house by 9 in the morning, that this affair might be further
concerted, and if possible money might be got out for answer-
ing the demand. And to prepare the way to the gate, a pass

and protection was to be obtain'd from the Prince, or from
Mr. Murray, as Secretary, for the directors and officers of the
Bank to go that length to try if the Governor would give
admittance. Mean time that a letter be prepared to be sent
to General Guest for notification, to be first transmitted to Mr.
Murray for his perusall to prevent all mistakes, and another
to the absent directors to acquaint them with this event,
that the directors present might be justified at the hands of
their constituents. Wrote to Lady G[lenorchy] and sent her
the Courant of this date, containing copy letters to the Royal
Burrows, to Collectors of the Land Tax of all the shires in
Scotland, and to the Collectors and Comptrollers of the Customs; and the Princes answer to the deputation from City of
Edinburgh about the message from the Castle, that unless the
communication with the town was opend they would fire
upon it.

                              Wednesday, 2d October.
     Messrs. Hamilton, Shairp, and Philp met at my house at
9 oclock agreable to appointment. Read over the Letters
prepared to be sent to General Guest and Mr. Murray. Indicted
a meeting of ordinary and extraordinary directors to meet at
my house at 12 oclock, for which purpose I made up and
signd printed notes for
          Mr. Hathorn and Mr. William Forbes,
          Mr. William Grant,
          Baillie Mansfield, and Mr. Keir.
All which notes were executed by Peter Campbell, officer, who
reported that only the first two were in town, and they came,
and when present with the above three ordinary directors
they all agreed to the measure proposd. Accordingly Mr.
David Baillie was sent to the Abbey with these two letters
which I signd and seald, and these he deliverd to Mr. Murray,
who return'd General Guest's letter, and added that there was
to be a further demand upon the Bank, the particulars whereof
he would acquaint me of as soon as possible. The directors
adjourn'd to dine at Mrs. Clerks to consider further of these
affairs; but first read and approv'd of the draught of a letter
to be dispatch'd to the absent directors to notify these resolu-

tions to them. 2 oClock. Dispatched James Lyon, porter,
to the Castle with my letter to General Guest, under safe-
guard from Lochiel per white flagg. Had a letter from St.
Germans, which I answered, thanking him for his kind invitation to me to go to his house to shun the calamity threatned
against the City of Edinburgh from the Castle. Sent Lady
Dunstaffnage by her boy 20 shillings in silver, and thank'd
her for her kind invitation to stay at her house during these
troubles. While at dinner at Mrs. Clerks about 3 oclock
afternoon, Mr. Peter Smith, brother to Methven, calld me to
another room and notified to me as Cashier that the Prince
had a further demand of current specie from the Royal Bank
for the sum of £2307 sterling of their notes, which he as
Attorney for his highness required payment of within 48
hours, under the penaltys containd in Mr. Murray of Brough-
tons former protest of yesterdays date, and exhibited the
Bank notes, in presence of W. Mackewan, notary publick,
before these witnesses   Writer to the Signet,
and   This further demand I immediatly
notified to the directors present in the next room, vizt. Messrs.
Hamilton, Shairp, Philp, Hathorn, and Forbes.   After
reasoning some time theron, they agreed to comply with this
demand, as well as the former, if access could be got to the
Castle. Some time after this, James Lyon, the porter, returned,
and brought back the letter for General Guest open, his
excellency having read the same, but did not incline to give a
written answer, not having a lawyer to advise with, but added
that if the directors had come in a private manner, they might
dispose of their own as they wou'd. After talking over this
matter a little Mr. Peter Smith calld me again, and presented
a pass to the Castle for the three ordinary directors and my
self, which pass was only to last and continue to this night at
10 oclock. I expostulated with him upon the impossibility
of the thing, but he said that all excuses was in vain, for that
a gentleman, who understood the business of banking, was
with the Prince, when the pass was agranting, who said that
there was no difficulty in the thing, for that all the gold and
silver must be in baggs of certain sums, and therefore that it
was an easy matter, and required no great time to execute this

affair, and so the Prince was positive to grant no longer indul-
gence. Hereupon Mr. Smith left me and I return'd to the
directors and reported what past, and being now towards
evening, they found the measure proposd by the pass imprac-
ticable, so adjourned to my house to drink coffee, and further
to deliberate of the affair. Bespoke a pott of coffee at Muirhead's. The directors talk'd over this exigency fully, and then
resolv'd that a letter should be written by me to Mr. Murray
of Broughton, desiring that the pass should be renewd for
to morrow, when they would try to get access to the Castle
and bring down the cash, and that the new pass should com-
prehend not only the three ordinary directors containd in the
former, viz\^t. Messrs. Hamilton, Shairp, and Philp and my self,
but likewise William Mitchell, accomptant, and Alexander
Innes, teller.   Accordingly I wrote a letter in these terms,
which was read to and approvd of by the meeting, and being
copied over fair by David Baillie (who had formerly tran-
scribed the other letters to General Guest and Mr. Murray of
Broughton in the forenoon), the same was sign'd by me, as the
other letters were, in presence of and by appointment of the
meeting.   On this the directors dismiss'd, and twas resolv'd
that the three ordinary directors, accomptant, and A. Innes,
teller, should meet at my house tomorrow between 8 and
9 in the morning.   But before the meeting was over, A.
Innes, teller, was calld upon, to know if his brother, George,
was in the Castle, who told he was not, on which he was dispatched to his house, to know if he had lodg'd the keys of the
Castle vault, where the Bank repositories were lodg'd, with his
wife, and if he had, to bring them, which accordingly he
deliverd to me in a seald parcell, which I opened in presence
of the directors, and then kept the keys, George Innes having
gone in to the countrey some days agoe, as his wife told his
brother.   Mr. David Baillie got the charge of delivering the
letter to Mr. Murray of Broughton, after sealing, but after all
search for him, he could not be found in town or abbey, on
which Mr. Baillie and I concerted that I should call for
Lochiel [1] in Mrs. Clerks, and tell him of the case, who brought

---

[1] Donald Cameron of Lochiel.   He escaped to France after Culloden.

me Mr. Smith who, with others, were in company with him, and in Lochiel's presence I deliverd the letter to Mr. Smith, who took burden to get and send me the answer this night. I then parted with these two gentlemen, all this discourse with them having past in the passage to Mrs. Clerks great room, and afterwards I went to John's Coffeehouse, where David Baillie waited me, to whom I told all that past, and then came home between 7 and 8 oclock. A little before parting with the directors I received a large packet from Lord Glenorchy per Jock, dated from Taymouth, 29 September, with letters inclosed

for Lady Glenorchy ⎫ all to be dispatched by
    Lady Harriet C. ⎬ to morrow's post.
    Philip Yorke, Esq. ⎭

I likewise received letter from Lord Monzie of the 29th September from Taymouth; also a letter from Auchalader same date from Taymouth, and one from his son John same date from Taymouth; all to be answered. Carwhins bill on me to Provost Fisher for 37 lb., dated 7 September @ 8 days date, was produced by George Chalmer, merchant in Leith, he having refused payment some days agoe in Bank notes of any kind. Between 10 and 11 at night a servant came to me with the pass to and from the Castle, which is limited between 8 in the morning and 3 afternoon to morrow.

Thursday, 3d October 1745.

About 7 this morning I wrote a letter to General Guest in the Castle acquainting him that Messrs. Jo. Hamilton, Alexander Shairp, and John Philip, directors of the Royal Bank, William Mitchel, accomptant, A. Innes, teller, and my self, as cashier, intended to go up to the Castle upon Bank business, therfore that he would please to give the proper orders to the Captain of the Guard to give us admittance upon our displaying a white flagg. This letter I sent up with James Lyon, porter, who us'd likewise a white napkin for his signall, and he reported we should be admitted. About 8 oclock the five gentlemen above nam'd met at my house, and after breakfast we proceeded on our expedition. This side of the Weigh house I calld for the Captain of the Highland guard (one Mr Cameron) to whom I shewd our pass, and after his reading the same, he calld for one of his men to go through all the centinells posted between that and the Reservoir to give them due notice, and after waiting about a quarter of an hour, the Captain desired us to proceed, for that all was safe before us. He kept the pass in his Custody to be deliverd to the next captain when he was relieved off guard. I then hoisted my white flag and ushered the rest of the gentlemen, saluting the centinells with it as we past, and as we approached the Castle gate wav'd it often. At last the centinells there calld to us to come forward, and on our arrival at the bridge, telling who we were, 'twas lett down ; the Captain received us in between the bridge and the gate, where he compard our names with my letter to General Guest which he had in his hand. On our arrival at General Guest's lodgings (which is the Governors new house) the directors and I went in, told him our errand in general was to get into the Royal Bank depositories to do some business, and General Preston having come in at that instant, he was likewise told the same. After some short conversation we left the two Generalls, and proceeded to the place where all the Bank things are lodg'd, and executed the affairs we came about, according to particular memorandums and minutes therof apart. During our continuance in the Castle which was from about 9 till near three oclock, there was closs firing from thence upon the Gardner's house at Livingston's yeards, occupied by R. Taylor, the shoemaker, at the head of a party of volunteers for the prince, to stop the communication thereabouts with the Castle, and one Watson, a soldier, was so couragious as to go down over the Castle wall upon a rope, fire upon the Gardners house, kill some of the volunteers there, carried off a firelock or two from them, sett the house in fire, return'd with these firelocks by his rope into the Castle, where he was received with loud huzzas for his valour. On his return the garrison was preparing for a sally, but as the men were a drawing up we got liberty from General Guest to go out again, and Captain Robert Mirry escorted us to the gate, where I again rais'd my white flagg, and with my friends return'd to town in safety, landed at my house from whence we adjournd to dine at Mrs. Clerks, vintner. No sooner were we sett down in Mrs. Clerks than we were inform'd that upon the sally from the Castle, Taylor and some of his men were taken and carried thither prisoners, leaving others dead on the spott, their house being sett on fire, the rest of the party having made their escape. Before I went to dinner I waited upon John Murray of Broughton, Esq., and told him I was come from the directors to acquaint him that they were ready to exchange current coin for their notes, in terms and in consequence of the two several demands made upon the Bank by way of protests and certification, on which he appointed six oclock at night to receive the money at my house, which I reported to the directors in Mrs. Clerks. After dinner I came down to make all ready and to keep the appointment, having packd up the gold in baggs to the net amount of the demands, being £3164.— About 7 oclock in place of Mr. Murrays coming himself, he sent one Mr Andrew Lumisdean (son to Wm. Lumisdean, writer, in Edinburgh), his depute secretary, who had with him the Bank notes. I told him the money was ready on the table, but that I hop'd he had the two protests duely discharg'd. He told me he had not, that they were of no moment, as they were never extended. On this we sent for Wm. M'Kewan, the notary, who acknowledged they were not drawn up, but tho' they were 'twas to Mr. Murray and not to me he was to deliver them; nor would Mr. Lumisdean promise to get them discharg'd, not knowing Mr. Murray's mind on that head. Being difficulted in this particular, and having no directors at hand to advise with, it was agreed, and Mr. M'Kewan promis'd faithfully to make out the protests against to morrow's morning to be deliverd to Mr. Murray, in case he should think proper to deliver them to the Bank. Hereupon I calld up A. Innes, teller, to compt over the Notes, and that being done, the gold was likewise told over, first by Mr. Innes, then by Mr. Mackewan, and last of all by Mr. Lumisdean, who put it up in several baggs, and these again in one large bag seald, which he caus'd carry up to his chair, and so we parted about eleven oclock at night, having drunk one bottle of wine during our business. Thereafter I lodged notes in their proper place in Bank. The net sum paid was 3076lb., Mr. Lumisdean having

disposed of £88 of the notes some other way. The Castle
continued firing on the Highland guards at the Weigh house.
When in the Castle today I deliverd two letters to General
Guest, the charge of which I had from John M'Farlane, Writer
to the Signet.

Friday, 4th October 1745.

Mr. Alexander Shairp calld upon me with a letter from Mr.
M'Culloch to the overseers of the Linnen Manufactory signifying the distress the work people were in for want of silver
coin, and desired I might assist him. The Castle has continued
firing most of this day and night on some of the uppermost
houses on the Castlehill, where the Highland guards shelterd
themselves, fired one of them, and some people kill'd near the
Weigh house. Had a message from J. G.[1] Secretary, by his
servant who left him at Alnwick, desiring me to look at some
papers his servant was to get in his scritore and to be sent to
him. He accordingly brought the papers, but without inspec-
tion I seald them up with his and my own seal to ly at my house
till further orders least they might be taken from the servant
on the road, as he was robbd in the morning, and wrote to Mr.
Graham accordingly, and desired him to send directions about
his furniture, etc., as James's Court where he lives is much
expos'd to the firing of the Castle.

Saturday, 5th October 1745.

Waited upon Mr. Murray of Broughton: desired from him
the protests taken by him against the Royal Bank. He
scroupled, as he saw no occasion for them. I added as one
principal reason for my asking them was that the repositories
were broke open when there was not a Court of Directors present, therefore in justification of all concerned 'twas necessary
to have them. He then gave his deputy, Mr. Lumsdean,
orders to cause the notary extend them, and on my return to
town I sent Mr. Mackewan a message to that purpose. Niccol,
the taylor, brought me my freeze coat, and I paid his account.
Answerd a letter of St. German's this forenoon. Constant
fireing from the Castle. Blocade taken off the Castle this
night by the Prince per printed notification to the inhabitants.

---

[1] Apparently J. Graham.

Sunday, 6th October 1745.

No sermon in the churches. Sent the Earl of Breadalbane the key of his little cabinet which lay by me seald since he fell ill, I say sent it seald to his lordship by his servant Allick. I was not abroad all this day.

Monday, 7th October.

I wrote to Auchallader telling I could not get his cloaths out of his taylors hands. Paid Jock 10 shillings, which with 6 shillings formerly is in full for going last time to Breadalbane, having gone the length of Tyndrom, and on his return 8 miles above Stirling, and besides freighting a yole in going, and got nothing while he continued in the countrey.

Tuesday, 8th October.

Calld for Lochiel about the letters deliverd me by Mr. John M'Farlane to General Guest, about Fassiefern's[1] imprisonment at Fort William, but miss'd Lochiel. Went to the Coffee house and read the news. On my way home met the accomptant and Robert Selkrig, teller, who came alongs, and I got the latter to sort all the Royal Bank notes I had got from Mr. Lumisdean in order to be ready for cancelling, and that being done lodged these notes back in their proper place. Dined at home *solus*. Had a message from Lochiel about the letters to General Guest, but could give him no answer other than that I deliverd them to the General as directed. Evening spent in making further progress in my minutes of Bank affairs.

Wednesday, 9 October 1745.

Waited upon Provost Coutts at his own house this morning, having sent me a message he was come to town. Went to John's Coffeehouse. Sent for William M'Kewan, notary, about Bank protests. On his coming, shewd me the protests duely sign'd, and inclosed them in a letter which was sent by my servant Allick, to Mr. Andrew Lumisdean at the Abbey, who promised to return them to me discharged very soon. Came home before dinner, and was calld upon by a servant of Sir Ch. Gs.[2] with whom I went to Pleasants and got two letters from Lady

---

[1] John Cameron of Fassifern.   [2] Not identified.

G[lenorchy]. Din'd at home *solus*. Lord Monzies house-maid calld at me for money to maintain her, and I gave her 10 shillings.

Thursday, 10th October 1745.

Went to the Coffeehouse. George Gordon calld upon me and told of the French ship landed at Montrose. Saw a letter of Lord Lovat's, about his Clan, etc., rising. Went to the Abbey and calld at Mr. Lumisdean for the two protests against the Royal Bank, who promised to send them to me to Earl Breadalbanes. Dined with Earl Breadalbane, Miss Boswell, Peggy Skene, and J[ohn] Murray. After dinner sent to Mr. Lumisdean for the Bank protests, which he sent me discharg'd. Earl Breadalbane gave me a letter and pass for his son to go to England, also a pass to John M'Diarmid to be sent with these to Taymouth. Sent letter to Lord M[onzie], and sent him Mercury of the 9th about Glenco, and discharging any members to go to parliament.

Friday, 11th October 1745.

Barclay, the taylor, brought me home Auchalader's cloaths.

Saturday, 12th October.

Sent to Lady Glenorchy the Prince's Declaration of the 10th addresst to all his fathers subjects.

Sunday, 13th October.

No sermon in churches. Dined with Earl Breadalbane, Taymouth, and Mr. John Murray. Came home in the evening.

Monday, 14th October 1745.

A meeting of directors. Present, Messrs. Shairp, Coutts, and Hamilton. Cancelld parcells of notes, vizt.

what I received from Broughton, ...	3076
what received from General Guest part of my balance, ...	600
	3676
more part of do. 20 shilling notes, . . .	1800

Calld a meeting of directors, ordinary and extraordinary; present, Messrs. Hamilton, Shairp, Coutts, Hathorn, Forbes,

and Mansfield. Dined at Mrs. Clerks and talkd over sundry
Bank business. Message per Bailie Mansfield to General
Guest for admittance about Bank business to the Castle—
agreed to. Meeting indicted for 9 to morrow. Officers of the
Bank came to me and I notified same. Had 1 bottle of wine.
Supp'd at Mr. Ronald Crawford's with sundrys.

Tuesday, 15th October 1745.

Coulterallers calld for loan of 6 guineas, which I gave him
on bill. Went to the Castle with Provost Coutts, David Baillie,
accomptant, and his clerk, Ewart, and three tellers about Bank
business, having notified our intention to General Guest, by a
letter which I wrote to him per Bailie Mansfield. Before we
went up had another crave for half crown contribution on Bank
house amounting to £8 : 2 : 6, which the directors agreed to
pay, so Bailie Mansfield was to advance it in my absence, and I
to repay him. Provost Coutts and I waited upon Generalls
Guest and Preston in the Castle. Then enterd upon our
business in the vault, vizt.—Settled and balanced the state of the
cash since 11 September. All the Bank notes cancell'd. The
tellers orderd to take down from the Castle all their balances.
All the notes formerly torn and not burnt, but laid up in the
directors old chest under lock, were this day burnt. All the
bills on 60 days, not formerly brought down, were deliverd to
David Baillie, his receipt or the Secretarys having formerly stood
for the same. All the foreign bills, and those from P. Murdoch,
etc. taken down by Robert Selkrig, in order to be lookt into.
On our coming from the Castle dined with Mr. Coutts, D.
Baillie and George Chalmers at Lucky Clerks, paid bill, 7
shillings. Went after dinner to the Castle with Mr. Coutts
and D. Baillie, and saw all the business finished. Came home,
Provost Coutts and D. Baillie with me, where the keys, seal,
and vouchers were seald up with Mr. Coutts's seall. Answered
Lady Glenorchy's letters of 8 and 10, but sent her nothing
enclosed, she having forbid to send any more newspapers. Got
a letter from Duncan Campbell. Answered letter of Lady
Dunstaffnage's [1] and sent her a guinea by her servant enclos'd.

---

[1] Wife of Neil Campbell of Dunstaffnage.

Wednesday, 16th October 1745.

Went to the Coffee house. Din'd *solus*. William Dow deliverd me a letter from Lady Glenorchy, dat'd 8, and another for Lord Glenorchy, both per express, but had been stopt on the road.

Thursday, 17th October.

Went to the Coffee house. Dined *solus*. Sent Auchalader Mercurys of 9 and 11, 14 and 16. Sent him his new friese cloaths. Answered Lady Glenorchy's of the 8th and 12. Told her all was well, quiet here, frequent reinforcements, ship landed at Montrose, one of distinction from thence lodges in Abbey.

Friday, 18 October 1745.

Robert Selkrig came to sort notes, which he finished. Messrs. Hamilton and Coutts mett and cancelled the same, per signd Inventary, agreable to which I'm to have credite in part of my balance, amounting to £6539. They afterwards came down to my house, where we had a glass of wine. A meeting of directors appointed against Monday at 10 o'clock.

Saturday, 19 October 1745.

Dined with Earl Breadalbane and Mr. John Murray at Abbey. Deliverd up all receipts I had from Finlay Murray for money advanced him for Earl Breadalbane. Returnd in a chair. Was calld upon after my return from the Abbey by one of Lord Tinwalds house-maids to tell that a son of Rollo of Powhouse was searching for arms at that lodging and at Lord Monzies, on which I went immediatly down, found him and his possie at Lord Tinwalds searching every corner, but he found nothing, he had a Highlander guarding the door with a drawn sword, from whom with difficulty I got access. Lord Monzies house-maid told me, they had taken two small swords out of Lord Monzie's per receipt, which she deliverd to me. Wrote to Lord Monzie under Lieut. James Campbell's cover, and acquainted him of the above search.

2 N

Sunday, 20 October 1745.

No sermon. Had a message from Earl Breadalbane to dine with him, but made my excuse.

Monday, 21 October 1745.

Messrs. Hamilton, Coutts, Shairp, and Philip mett at the Bank according to appointment. Went through the forreign bills, and gave sign'd directions concerning the same. Deliverd to David Baillie all the 60 day bills upon receipt in order to protest and registrat them before expiry, his and the Secretary's receipts standing already for the former parcells in his hands. Patrick Smyth, brother to Methven, made a demand in the Prince's name, for payment of £1819 Royal Bank notes in current coin between and Wednesday at 12 oclock, and took instruments therupon in hands of   · Watson, notary, before Andrew Porteous of Burnfoot and Andrew Swan, in-dwellers in Edinburgh, witnesses. This demand was imme-diatly notified to the directors, sitting in the Bank office, who orderd that the same should be comply'd with. Dined with Earl Breadalbane, Messrs. William and John Murray at the Abbey. Waited on Broughton that he might appoint an hour for geting payment of Mr. Smith's demand, and he nam'd about five this evening. Broughton according to appointment sent his deputy, Mr. Lumisdean, with the Royal Bank notes, which Robert Selkrig received off his hand, and then told over the gold to him, amounting to £1819, which he scald up in his bags and carried away with him. Had a bottle of wine. I got up the protest taken against the Bank from Mr. Lumisdean discharg'd by Mr. Murray of Broughton, and as Swan, one of the witnesses, could not be had to sign the same, Mr. Lumisdean is to send him to me to morrow for that purpose.

Tuesday, 22d October 1745.

Had a letter from St. Germans, which I answered. Dined at D. Anderson's with D. Baillie.

Wednesday, 23d October 1745.

Received payment of Mr. Jo. Philp payment of the £8 he owd me. Gave him £10 in silver out of the Bank balance per

draught on Bank of £18, in which is included the above £8.
Call'd at John M'Kenzie, writer, about Earl Eglintones bills in
Bank, and Bond of Corroborate he was to grant for the largest
—Mr. M'Kenzie not being in town, his clerk, Mr. Gray, told
me the bond was sign'd, and would be deliverd up on Mr.
M'Kenzies return to town next week. And for the bills a
letter might be written to Earl Eglintone to the care of the
postmaster of Irvine. Dind at home *solus*.

Thursday, 24th October.

A further demand was this morning early made by Mr.
Lumisdean in name of the Prince for the sum of £1117 to
be paid in current coin in exchange for notes. The foregoing demand I immediatly notified to Messrs. Hamilton and
Philp, who came to the Bank at a call, who agreed to comply,
and Mr. Lumisdean has appointed 6 at night for receiving
the money. Had a message from the Old Bank desiring to
exchange all our notes in their hands, and in as far as they
were short of what we had of theirs would give cash to make
up the balance. Mr. Lumisdean came and got £1117 in gold
for Royal Bank notes. George Stirling calld this night and
supp'd with me. Indicted a meeting of directors to morrow at
12 oclock about the message from the Old Bank, etc.

Friday, 25th October 1745.

Paid M'Diarmid 9 shillings, which, with 6 shillings formerly,
completes his last journey to Breadalbane. A. Innes, senior,
breakfasted with me. The accomptant calld at me. Had a
letter to Lady Veronica Campbell's burial. Directors met and
resolv'd to exchange 4000 £ notes with Old Bank to morrow.
Had a message from Old Bank by Messrs. Fairholm and Spence
to exchange the notes within the Castle, which I told them
could not be comply'd with, as the notes we had of theirs were
brought from thence.—Had a bottle wine at my house with
them.

Saturday, 26th October 1745.

Mungo Roro calld at me and breakfasted. George Stirling
came and took leave. Mr. Spence calld to tell that the
Old Bank directors had agreed to exchange the 4000lb. notes
at Mr. Fairholm's house at 2 oclock, which I notified to Mr.

Selkrig that he might attend. Mr. Kinloch's servant-maid came to acquaint me that her masters house at Bruntfield Links was robbd and pillaged last night by 15 Highlanders and 2 women, but knew none of their names. I beged of Mungo Roro to get all the information he could, and if possible to recover the goods that the rogues might be punished, which he undertook so far as lay in his power. Mr. Kinloch's maid is to endeavour to bring me further information. D. Baillie dined with me. Exchang'd £4000 notes with the Old Bank. While at dinner Mr. Lumisden sent me a message he was to call in the afternoon, accordingly at 3 oclock he came and protested £417 Royal Bank notes, and having afterwards called I gave him £400 in gold, with which he was satisfied, having restricted his demand to that sum. Had a letter from Auchalader, who is a dying, dated 22d. Earl Breadalbane calld upon me to the Abbey, went down in a chair, suppd with his lordship and Mr. John Murray. Returnd in a chair, paid 2 shillings and 1 shilling to the Earl's servant who conducted me backward and forward.

Sunday, 27 October 1745.

No sermon. Went to the Castle, deliverd the letters for General Guest from Lord Glenorchy and Governor Alexander Campbell and message from Lord Monzie all about Fassiefern, but the General would not give answers in writing, only verbally, that he thought the Governor might release him on good bail such as Lord Glenorchy approvd of. Returnd to the Coffeehouse. Dined at home *solus*. Inshewen [1] calld upon me after dinner, to whom I deliverd Auchaladers letter about his son, Peter. Letters came to me from the Abbey for my dispatching Anderston to Taymouth.

Monday, 28th October 1745.

Court of Directors ordinary and extraordinary.

Present.

Ordinary.	Extraordinary.
Mr. Hamilton.	Mr. Hathorn.
Mr. Shairp.	Mr. Forbes.
Mr. Philp.	Mr. Mansfield.

[1] John Ogilvy of Inshewan in Forfarshire.

Had under consideration a letter from Mr. Coutts to Mr. Hamilton, advising that upon a conversation with the Lord Justice Clerk about Bank affairs, his lordship had found fault with almost every part of the directors conduct, but had not time to give the particulars. As the directors were not sensible of any one article of misconduct, they delayed saying any thing further of that matter till Mr. Hamilton should have another letter from Provost Coutts. The Cashier retorted that he had exchangd £4000 Old Bank notes for new. It was the opinion of the meeting that as many old notes as possible should be got, and that they themselves should contribute what they could that way. It was further their opinion that in case any after demand should be made upon the Bank by the Prince within £2000, that the same should be answerd as formerly, and that the ordinary directors shoud take the same out of the Castle. Agreed to take payments from Mr. Coutts of the 4000£ Bank money in his hands, as money comes in to him, but that his partner should be told that specie or old Bank notes would be more acceptable. Made up Bank Minutes to this day. Poem.

Tuesday, 29th October 1745.

Had a confused story of a forgery of the Royal Bank notes, which was told him by John Bisset, whom I sent for, and he's to bring all the information he can get. Dined at home *solus*. Poem continued.

Wednesday, 30 October 1745.

Mr. Lumisden made a further demand of £174 to be exchangd tomorrow at 12 oclock. Sent snuff and paper to Earl Breadalbane.

Thursday, 31 October.

Exchangd some Royal for old Bank notes with Bailie Mansfield. Dined *solus*. The Prince went this evening to Pinkie.

Friday, 1 November 1745.

Mr. Lumisdean calld for 174 lb. in gold for notes of like value, but had not the protest extended, the notary and wit-

nesses having left the town, and Broughton was likewise gone.
Mr. Trotter calld at me from Provost Coutts to know if I had
any message for him. Told him the directors were willing to
take what partial payments he could conveniently make.
Dined *solus.* Highlanders left this place wholly today.

Saturday, 2d November 1745.
To Lieutenant James Campbell I notified that the City was
thinner than for some weeks past.

Sunday, 3 November.
Heard sermon per Mathison, new Church. Din'd with Earl
Breadalbane and James Holburn and John Murray at Abbey.
Sup'd with Earl Breadalbane. Returnd in a Chair.

Monday, 4 November 1745.
Had a Letter from the Earl of Breadalbane telling me
the mob had got up in the Abbey, were opening doors, and
like to destroy the house and every thing in it, therefore desiring to apply to General Guest for a safe guard, and to shew
him his lordship's letter. Accordingly I wrote to the General.
Sent the Earls letter inclosed by Finlay Moray, that he might
tell the General what he had seen. Finlay Moray return'd
and told me the General was immediatly to send down a guard
to the Abbey to protect it.

Wednesday, 6th November 1745.
Mr. Kinlochs maid calld upon me for a letter to Mr.
Glasgow in the Castle to be assisting to her in finding out the
things pillag'd out of her masters house amongst these carried
up to the Castle. Dined at Abbey with Earl Breadalbane, St.
Germans, and Mr. John Murray. St. Germans treated me
with a coach to the Abbey and back again. Supp'd at home,
St. Germans with me.

Monday, 11 November 1745.
Din'd at home *solus.* Began to compose some lines. Paid
a visit at Mr. Kinloch's. Finish'd my composure.

Wednesday, 13 November 1745.

Wrote to Miss Jenny, and sent her gloves and snuff and returnd her key. Exchanged new for old notes with Bailie Mansfield, 215. This day the Judges enterd the City in procession.

Thursday, 14 November 1745.

2000 foot and dragoons enterd the City this evening.

Monday, 18 November 1745.

Wrote to Lord Justice Clerk about Bank affairs, and advised him the old Bank had opend shop.

Wednesday, 20 November 1745.

Went to the Castle of Edinburgh with severall of the officers of the Bank, and got down all the boxes belonging to the accomptants office, being 18 in number.

Saturday, 23 November 1745.

Got down rest of Bank effects from Castle.

Scottish History Society

———◆———

LIST OF MEMBERS

NOVEMBER 6, 1893.

LIST OF MEMBERS

Abernethy, James, 11 Prince of Wales Terrace, Kensington, London, W.

Adam, Sir Charles E., Bart., Blair-Adam.

Adam, Robert, Brae-Moray, Gillsland Road, Edinburgh.

Adam, Thomas, Hazelbank, Uddingston.

Adams, William, 28 Ashton Terrace, Hillhead, Glasgow.

Agnew, Alex., Procurator-Fiscal, Court-House Buildings, Dundee.

Aikman, Andrew, 27 Buckingham Terrace, Edinburgh.

Aitken, Dr. A. P., 57 Great King Street, Edinburgh.

Aitken, James H., Gartcows, Falkirk.

10 Alexander, William, M.D., Dundonald, Kilmarnock.

Allan, A. G., Blackfriars Haugh, Elgin.

Allan, George, Advocate, 56 Castle Street, Aberdeen.

Anderson, Archibald, 30 Oxford Square, London, W.

Anderson, Arthur, M.D., C.B., Sunny-Brae, Pitlochry.

Anderson, John, jun., Atlantic Mills, Bridgeton, Glasgow.

Andrew, Thomas, Doune, Perthshire.

Armstrong, Robert Bruce, 6 Randolph Cliff, Edinburgh.

Arnot, James, M.A., 57 Leamington Terrace, Edinburgh.

Arrol, William A., 11 Lynedoch Place, Glasgow.

20 Baird, J. G. A., Wellwood, Muirkirk.

Balfour, C. B., Newton Don, Kelso.

Balfour, Right Hon. J. B., Q.C., 6 Rothesay Terrace, Edinburgh.

Ballingall, Hugh, Ardarroch, Dundee.

Barclay, George, 17 Coates Crescent, Edinburgh.

Barclay R., Bury Hill, Dorking.

Barron, Rev. Douglas Gordon, Dunnottar Manse, Stonehaven.

Begg, Ferdinand Faithfull, 13 Earl's Court Square, London, S.W.

Bell, A. Beatson, Advocate, 2 Eglinton Crescent, Edinburgh.

Bell, Joseph, F.R.C.S., 2 Melville Crescent, Edinburgh.

30 Bell, Robert Fitzroy, Advocate, 7 Ainslie Place, Edinburgh.

Bell, Russell, Advocate, Kildalloig, Campbeltown.

Beveridge, Erskine, St. Leonard's Hill, Dunfermline.

Black, James Tait, 33 Palace Court, Bayswater Hill, London, W.

Black, Rev. John S., 6 Oxford Terrace, Edinburgh.

Blaikie, Walter B., 11 Thistle Street, Edinburgh.

Blair, Patrick, Advocate, 4 Ardross Terrace, Inverness.

Bonar, Horatius, W.S., 15 Strathearn Place, Edinburgh.

Boyd, Sir Thomas J., 41 Moray Place, Edinburgh.

Brodie, Sir T. D., Bart., W.S., 5 Thistle Street, Edinburgh.

40 Brookman, James, W.S., 16 Ravelston Park, Edinburgh.

Broun-Morison, J. B., of Finderlie, The Old House, Harrow-on-the-Hill.

Brown, Professor Alex. Crum, 8 Belgrave Crescent, Edinburgh.

Brown, J. A. Harvie, Dunipace House, Larbert, Stirlingshire.

Brown, P. Hume, 25 Gillespie Crescent, Edinburgh.

Brown, Robert, Underwood Park, Paisley.

Brown, William, 26 Princes Street, Edinburgh.

Brownlie, James R., 10 Brandon Pl., West George St., Glasgow.

Bruce, Alex., Clyne House, Sutherland Avenue, Pollokshields.

Bruce, James, W.S., 23 St. Bernard's Crescent, Edinburgh.

50 Bruce, Hon. R. Preston, Broom Hall, Dunfermline.

Bryce, James, M.P., 54 Portland Place, London, W.

Bryce, William Moir, 5 Dick Place, Edinburgh.

Buchanan, A. W. Gray, Parkhill, Polmont, N.B.

Buchanan, T. D., M.D., 24 Westminster Terrace, West, Glasgow.

Burns, Rev. George Stewart, D.D., 3 Westbourne Terrace, Glasgow.

Burns, John William, Kilmahew, Cardross.

Burns, Rev. Thomas, 2 St. Margaret's Road, Edinburgh.

Bute, The Marquis of, Mountstuart, Isle of Bute.

CALDWELL, JAMES, Craigielea Place, Paisley.
60 Cameron, Dr. J. A., Nairn.
Cameron, Richard, 1 South St. David Street, Edinburgh.
Campbell, Rev. James, D.D., the Manse, Balmerino, Dundee.
Campbell, James A., Stracathro, Brechin.
Campbell, P. W., W.S., 49 Melville Street, Edinburgh.
Carmichael, Sir Thomas D. Gibson, Bart., Castlecraig, Dolphinton, N.B.
Carne-Ross, Joseph, M.D., Parsonage Nook, Withington, Manchester.
Carrick, J. Stewart, 58 Renfield Street, Glasgow.
Chambers, W. & R., 339 High Street, Edinburgh.
Chiene, Professor, 26 Charlotte Square, Edinburgh.
70 Christie, J., Breadalbane Estate Office, Kenmore, Aberfeldy.
Christie, Thomas Craig, of Bedlay, Chryston, Glasgow.
Clark, George T., Talygarn, Llantrissant.
Clark, James, Advocate, 4 Drumsheugh Gardens, Edinburgh.
Clark, James T., Crear Villa, Ferry Road, Edinburgh.
Clark, Robert, 42 Hanover Street, Edinburgh.
Clark, Sir Thomas, Bart., 11 Melville Crescent, Edinburgh.
Clouston, T. S., M.D., Tipperlinn House, Morningside Place, Edinburgh.
Cochran-Patrick, R. W., LL.D., of Woodside, Beith, Ayrshire.
Constable, Archibald, 11 Thistle Street, Edinburgh.
80 Cowan, George, 1 Gillsland Road, Edinburgh.
Cowan, Hugh, St. Leonards, Ayr.
Cowan, J. J., 38 West Register Street, Edinburgh.
Cowan, John, W.S., St. Roque, Grange Loan, Edinburgh.
Cowan, John, Beeslack, Mid-Lothian.
Cowan, William, 2 Montpelier, Edinburgh.
Craik, James, W.S., 9 Eglinton Crescent, Edinburgh.
Crawford, Donald, M.P., 60 Pall Mall, London.
Crole, Gerard L., Advocate, 30 Northumberland Street, Edinburgh.
Cunningham, Geo. Miller, C.E., 2 Ainslie Place, Edinburgh.
90 Cunynghame, R. J. Blair, M.D., 18 Rothesay Place, Edinburgh.

Curle, James, W.S., Priorwood, Melrose.

Currie, James, 16 Bernard Street, Leith.

Currie, Walter Thomson, Rankeillour, by Cupar-Fife.

Currie, W. R., 30 Burnbank Gardens, Glasgow.

Cuthbert, Alex. A., 14 Newton Terrace, Glasgow.

DALGLEISH, JOHN J., Brankston Grange, Bogside Station, Stirling.

Dalrymple, Hon. Hew, Lochinch, Castle Kennedy, Wigtownshire.

Davidson, Hugh, Braedale, Lanark.

Davidson, J., Solicitor, Kirriemuir.

100 Davidson, Thomas, 339 High Street, Edinburgh.

Davies, J. Mair, C.A., Sheiling, Pollokshields, Glasgow.

Dickson, Thomas, LL.D., Register House, Edinburgh.

Dickson, Dr. Walter G. W., 3 Royal Circus, Edinburgh.

Dickson, William K., Advocate, 19 Dundas Street, Edinburgh.

Dickson, Wm. Traquair, W.S., 11 Hill Street, Edinburgh.

Dixon, John H., Inveran, Poolewe, by Dingwall.

Doak, Rev. Andrew, M.A., 15 Queen's Road, Aberdeen.

Dodds, Rev. James, D.D., The Manse, Corstorphine.

Dods, Colonel P., United Service Club, Edinburgh.

110 Donald, C. D., 172 St. Vincent Street, Glasgow.

Donaldson, James, LL.D., Principal, St. Andrews University.

Donaldson, James, Sunnyside, Formby, Liverpool.

Douglas, Hon. and Right Rev. A. G., Bishop of Aberdeen and Orkney, Aberdeen.

Douglas, David, 9 Castle Street, Edinburgh.

Dowden, Right Rev. John, D.D., Bishop of Edinburgh, Lynn House, Gillsland Road, Edinburgh.

Duff, T. Gordon, Drummuir, Keith.

Duncan, James Barker, W.S., 6 Hill Street, Edinburgh.

Duncan, John, National Bank, Haymarket, Edinburgh.

Dundas, Ralph, C.S., 28 Drumsheugh Gardens, Edinburgh.

120 Dunn, Robert Hunter, Belgian Consulate, Glasgow.

EASTON, WALTER, 125 Buchanan Street, Glasgow.

Ewart, Prof. Cossar, 2 Belford Park, Edinburgh.

FAULDS, A. WILSON, Knockbuckle, Beith, Ayrshire.

Ferguson, James, Advocate, 10 Wemyss Place, Edinburgh.

Ferguson, John, Town Clerk, Linlithgow.

Ferguson, Rev. John, Manse, Aberdalgie, Perth.

Findlay, J. Ritchie, 3 Rothesay Terrace, Edinburgh.

Findlay, Rev. Wm., The Manse, Saline, Fife.

Firth, Charles Harding, 33 Norham Road, Oxford.

130 Fleming, D. Hay, 16 North Bell Street, St. Andrews.

Fleming, J. S., 16 Grosvenor Crescent, Edinburgh.

Flint, Prof., D.D., LL.D., Johnstone Lodge, Craigmillar Park, Edinburgh.

Forrest, James R. P., 32 Broughton Place, Edinburgh.

Forrester, John, 29 Windsor Street, Edinburgh.

Foulis, James, M.D., 34 Heriot Row, Edinburgh.

Fraser, Professor A. Campbell, D.C.L., LL.D., Gorton House, Hawthornden.

GAIRDNER, CHARLES, Broom, Newton-Mearns, Glasgow.

Galletly, Edwin G., 7 St. Ninian's Terrace, Edinburgh.

Gardiner, Samuel, LL.D., South View, Widmore Road, Bromley, Kent.

140 Gardner, Alexander, 7 Gilmour Street, Paisley.

Gartshore, Miss Murray, Ravelston, Blackhall, Edinburgh.

Geikie, Sir Archibald, LL.D., Geological Survey, 28 Jermyn Street, London, S.W.

Geikie, Prof. James, LL.D., 31 Merchiston Avenue, Edinburgh.

Gemmill, William, 62 Bath Street, Glasgow.

Gibson, Andrew, 3 Morrison Street, Govan.

Gibson, James T., LL.B., W.S., 28 St. Andrew Sq., Edinburgh.

Giles, Arthur, 107 Princes Street, Edinburgh.

Gillespie, Mrs. G. R., Advocate, 5 Darnaway Street, Edinburgh.

Gillies, Walter, M.A., The Academy, Perth.

150 Gordon, Rev. Robert, Mayfield Gardens, Edinburgh.

Goudie, Gilbert, F.S.A.Scot., 39 Northumberland St., Edinburgh.

Goudie, James Tulloch, Oakleigh Park, Nithsdale Drive, Pollokshields.

Goudie, Robert, Commissary Clerk of Ayrshire, Ayr.

Gourlay, Robert, Bank of Scotland, Glasgow.

Gow, Leonard, Hayston, Kelvinside, Glasgow.

Graeme, Lieut.-Col. R. C., Naval and Military Club, 94 Piccadilly, London.

Grahame, James, 93 Hope Street, Glasgow.

Grant, William G. L., Woodside, East Newport, Fife.

Gray, George, Clerk of the Peace, Glasgow.

160 Greig, Andrew, 36 Belmont Gardens, Hillhead, Glasgow.

Gunning, His Excellency Robert Haliday, M.D., 12 Addison Crescent, Kensington, London, W.

Guthrie, Charles J., Advocate, 13 Royal Circus, Edinburgh.

Guy, Robert, 120 West Regent Street, Glasgow.

HALKETT. MISS KATHERINE E., 2 Edinburgh Terrace, Kensington, London, W.

Hall, David, Elmbank House, Kilmarnock.

Hallen, Rev. A. W. Cornelius, The Parsonage, Alloa.

Hamilton, Hubert, Advocate, 55 Manor Place, Edinburgh.

Hamilton, Lord, of Dalzell, Motherwell.

Hamilton-Ogilvy, Henry T. N., Prestonkirk.

170 Harrison, John, 36 North Bridge, Edinburgh.

Hedderwick, A. W. H., 79 St. George's Place, Glasgow.

Henderson, J. G. B., Nether Parkley, Linlithgow.

Henderson, Joseph, 11 Blythswood Square, Glasgow.

Henry, David, 2 Lockhart Place, St. Andrews, Fife.

Hewison, Rev. J. King, The Manse, Rothesay.

Hill, William H., LL.D., Barlanark, Shettleston, Glasgow.

Hogg, John, 66 Chancery Street, Boston, U.S.

Honeyman, John, A.R.S.A., 140 Bath Street, Glasgow.

Howden, Charles R. A., Advocate, 25 Melville Street, Edinburgh.

180 Hunter, Colonel, F.R.S., of Plâs Côch, Anglesea.

Hutcheson, Alexander, Herschel House, Broughty Ferry.

Hutchison, Rev. John, D.D., Afton Lodge, Bonnington.

Hyslop, J. M., M.D., 22 Palmerston Place, Edinburgh.

Imrie, Rev. T. Nairne, Dunfermline.

Jameson, J. H., W.S., 3 Northumberland Street, Edinburgh.

Jamieson, George Auldjo, C.A., 37 Drumsheugh Gardens, Edinburgh.

Jamieson, J. Auldjo, W.S., 14 Buckingham Ter., Edinburgh.

Johnston, David, 24 Huntly Gardens, Kelvinside, Glasgow.

Johnston, George Harvey, 6 Osborne Terrace, Edinburgh.

190 Johnston, George P., 33 George Street, Edinburgh.

Johnston, T. Morton, Eskhill, Roslin.

Johnstone, James F. Kellas, 3 Broad Street Buildings, Liverpool Street, London.

Jonas, Alfred Charles, Poundfald, Penclawdd, Swansea.

Kemp, D. William, Ivy Lodge, Trinity, Edinburgh.

Kennedy, David H. C., 69 St. George's Place, Glasgow.

Kermack, John, W.S., 10 Atholl Crescent, Edinburgh.

Kincairney, The Hon. Lord, 6 Heriot Row, Edinburgh.

Kinnear, The Hon. Lord, 2 Moray Place, Edinburgh.

Kirkpatrick, Prof. John, LL.D., Advocate, 24 Alva Street, Edinburgh.

200 Kirkpatrick, Robert, 1 Queen Square, Strathbungo, Glasgow.

Laidlaw, David, jun., 6 Marlborough Ter., Kelvinside, Glasgow.

Laing, Alex., Norfolk House, St. Leonards, Sussex.

Lang, James, 9 Crown Gardens, Dowanhill, Glasgow.

Langwill, Robert B., The Manse, Currie.

Laurie, Professor S. S., Nairne Lodge, Duddingston.

Law, James F., Seaview, Monifieth.

Law, Thomas Graves, Signet Library, Edinburgh, *Secretary*.

Leadbetter, Thomas, 122 George Street, Edinburgh.

Leslie, Lieut.-Colonel, Cameron Highlanders, Malta.

210 Livingston, E. B., 9 Gracechurch Street, London, E.C.

Lorimer, George, 2 Abbotsford Crescent, Edinburgh.

Macadam, W. Ivison, Slioch, Lady Road, Newington, Edinburgh.

M'Alpine, William, 11 Archibald Place, Edinburgh.

Macandrew, Sir Henry C., Aisthorpe, Midmills Road, Inverness.

Macbrayne, David, Jun., 17 Royal Exchange Square, Glasgow.

M'Candlish, John M., W.S., 27 Drumsheugh Gar., Edinburgh.

M'Cosh, J. M., Clydesdale Bank, Dalry, Ayrshire.

Macdonald, James, W.S., 4 Greenhill Park, Edinburgh.

Macdonald, W. Rae, 1 Forres Street, Edinburgh.

220 Macdougall, Jas. Patten, Advocate, 16 Lynedoch Pl., Edinburgh.

M'Ewen, W. C., W.S., 2 Rothesay Place, Edinburgh.

Macfarlane, Geo. L., Advocate, 3 St. Colme Street, Edinburgh.

Macgeorge, B. B., 19 Woodside Crescent, Glasgow.

Macgregor, John, W.S., 10 Dundas Street, Edinburgh.

M'Grigor, Alexander, 172 St. Vincent Street, Glasgow.

Macintyre, P. M., Advocate, 12 India Street, Edinburgh.

Mackay, Æneas J. G., LL.D., 7 Albyn Place, Edinburgh.

Mackay, Eneas, 43 Murray Place, Stirling.

Mackay, Rev. G. S., M.A., Free Church Manse, Doune.

230 Mackay, James F., W.S., Whitehouse, Cramond.

Mackay, James R., 37 St. Andrew Square, Edinburgh.

Mackay, John, Elisabethan Strasse 15, Wiesbaden, Germany.

Mackay, Thomas, 14 Wetherby Place, South Kensington, London, S.W.

Mackay, Thomas A., 14 Henderson Row, Edinburgh.

Mackay, William, Solicitor, Inverness.

Mackenzie, A., St. Catherines, Paisley.

Mackenzie, David J., Sheriff-Substitute, Wick.

Mackenzie, Thomas, M.A., Sheriff-Substitute of Ross, Old Bank, Golspie.

Mackinlay, David, 6 Great Western Terrace, Glasgow.

240 Mackinnon, Professor, 1 Merchiston Place, Edinburgh.

Mackintosh, Charles Fraser, 5 Clarges Street, London, W.

Mackintosh, W. F., 27 Commerce Street, Arbroath.

Maclachan, John, W.S., 12 Abercromby Place, Edinburgh.

Maclagan, Prof. Sir Douglas, M.D., 28 Heriot Row, Edinburgh.

Maclagan, Robert Craig, M.D., 5 Coates Crescent, Edinburgh.

Maclauchlan, John, Albert Institute, Dundee.

Maclean, Sir Andrew, Viewfield House, Balshagray, Partick, Glasgow.

Maclean, William C., F.R.G.S., 31 Camperdown Place, Great Yarmouth.

MacLehose, James J., 61 St. Vincent Street, Glasgow.

250 Macleod, Rev. Walter, 112 Thirlestane Road, Edinburgh.

Macphail, J. R. N., Advocate, 53 Castle Street, Edinburgh.

M'Phee, Donald, Oakfield, Fort William.

Macray, Rev. W. D., Bodleian Library, Oxford.

Macritchie, David, 4 Archibald Place, Edinburgh.

Main, W. D., 128 St. Vincent Street, Glasgow.

Makellar, Rev. William, 8 Charlotte Square, Edinburgh.

Marshall, John, Caldergrove, Newton, Lanarkshire.

Martin, Francis John, W.S., 9 Glencairn Crescent, Edinburgh.

Marwick, Sir J. D., LL.D., Killermont Ho., Maryhill, Glasgow.

260 Masson, Professor David, I.L.D., 34 Melville St., Edinburgh.

Mathieson, Thomas A., 3 Grosvenor Terrace, Glasgow.

Maxwell, W. J., M.P., Terraughtie, Dumfries.

Melville, Viscount, Melville Castle, Lasswade.

Millar, Alexander H., Rosslyn House, Clepington Rd., Dundee.

Miller, P., 8 Bellevue Terrace, Edinburgh.

Milligan, John, W.S., 10 Carlton Terrace, Edinburgh.

Milne, A. & R., Union Street, Aberdeen.

Mitchell, Rev. Prof. Alexander, D.D., University, St. Andrews.

Mitchell, Sir Arthur, K.C.B., M.D., LL.D., 34 Drummond Place, Edinburgh.

270 Mitchell, James, 240 Darnley Street, Pollokshields, Glasgow.

Moncrieff, W. G. Scott, Advocate, Weedingshall Ho., Polmont.

Moffatt, Alexander, 23 Abercromby Place, Edinburgh.

Moffatt, Alexander, jun., M.A., LL.B., Advocate, 45 Northumberland Street, Edinburgh.

Morice, Arthur D., Fonthill Road, Aberdeen.

Morison, John, 11 Burnbank Gardens, Glasgow.

Morries-Stirling, J. M., Gogar House, Stirling.

Morrison, Hew, 7 Hermitage Terrace, Morningside.

Muir, James, 27 Huntly Gardens, Dowanhill, Glasgow.

Muirhead, James, 10 Doune Gardens, Kelvinside, Glasgow.

280 Murdoch, Rev. A. D., All Saints' Parsonage, Edinburgh.

Murdoch, J. B., of Capelrig, Mearns, Renfrewshire.

Murray, Rev. Allan F., M.A., Free Church Manse, Torphichen, Bathgate.

Murray, David, 169 West George Street, Glasgow.

Norfor, Robert T., C.A., 30 Morningside Drive, Edinburgh.

Ogilvy, Sir Reginald, Bart., Baldovan, Dundee.

Oliver, James, Thornwood, Hawick.

Orrock, Archibald, 17 St. Catherine's Place, Edinburgh.

Panton, George A., F.R.S.E., 73 Westfield Road, Edgbaston, Birmingham.

Paton, Allan Park, Greenock Library, Watt Monument, Greenock.

290 Paton, Henry, M.A., 15 Myrtle Terrace, Edinburgh.

Patrick, David, 339 High Street, Edinburgh.

Paul, J. Balfour, Advocate, Lyon King of Arms, 30 Heriot Row, Edinburgh.

Paul, Rev. Robert, F.S.A. Scot., Dollar.

Pearson, David Ritchie, M.D., 23 Upper Phillimore Place, Phillimore Gardens, London, W.

Pillans, Hugh H., 12 Dryden Place, Edinburgh.

Pollock, Hugh, 25 Carlton Place, Glasgow.

Prentice, A. R., 18 Kilblain Street, Greenock.

Pullar, Robert, Tayside, Perth.

Purves, A. P., W.S., Esk Tower, Lasswade.

300 Ramage, John, Hillbank Cottage, Thistle Street, Dundee.

Rankine, John, Advocate, Professor of Scots Law, 23 Ainslie Place, Edinburgh.

Reichel, H. R., Principal, University College, Bangor, North Wales.

Reid, Alexander George, Solicitor, Auchterarder.

Reid, H. G., 11 Cromwell Cres., S. Kensington, London, S.W.
Reid, John Alexander, Advocate, 11 Royal Circus, Edinburgh.
Renwick, Robert, Depute Town-Clerk, City Chambers, Glasgow.
Richardson, Ralph, W.S., Commissary Office, 2 Parliament
    Square, Edinburgh.
Ritchie, David, Hopeville, Dowanhill Gardens, Glasgow.
Ritchie, R. Peel, M.D., 1 Melville Crescent, Edinburgh.
310 Roberton, James D., 1 Park Terrace East, Glasgow.
Robertson, D. Argyll, M.D., 18 Charlotte Square, Edinburgh.
Robertson, J. Stewart, W.S., Edradynate, Ballinluig.
Robertson, John, Elmslea, Dundee.
Robson, William, Marchholm, Gillsland Road, Edinburgh.
Rogerson, John J., LL.B., Merchiston Castle, Edinburgh.
Rosebery, The Earl of, K.G., Dalmeny Park, Linlithgowshire.
Ross, T. S., Balgillo Terrace, Broughty Ferry.
Ross, Rev. William, LL.D., 7 Grange Terrace, Edinburgh.
Ross, Rev. William, Partick, Glasgow.
320 Russell, John, 7 Seton Place, Edinburgh.

Scott, Rev. Archibald, D.D., 16 Rothesay Place, Edinburgh.
Scott, John, C.B., Seafield, Greenock.
Shaw, David, W.S., 1 Thistle Court, Edinburgh.
Shaw, Rev. R. D., B.D., 21 Lauder Road, Edinburgh.
Shaw, Thomas, M.P., Advocate, 17 Abercromby Pl., Edinburgh.
Shiell, John, 5 Bank Street, Dundee.
Shiells, Robert, National Bank of Neenah, Neenah, Wisconsin.
Simpson, Prof. A. R., 52 Queen Street, Edinburgh.
Simpson, Sir W. G., Bart., Balabraes, Ayton, Berwickshire.
330 Simson, D. J., Advocate, 3 Glenfinlas Street, Edinburgh.
Sinclair, Alexander, Glasgow Herald Office, Glasgow.
Skelton, John, Advocate, C.B., LL.D., the Hermitage of
    Braid, Edinburgh.
Skinner, William, W.S., 35 George Square, Edinburgh.
Smail, Adam, 13 Cornwall Street, Edinburgh.
Smart, William, M.A., Nunholm, Dowanhill, Glasgow.
Smith, Andrew, Broompark, Lanark.

Smith, G. Gregory, M.A., 9 Warrender Park Cres., Edinburgh.
Smith, Rev. G. Mure, 6 Clarendon Place, Stirling.
Smith, Rev. R. Nimmo, Manse of the First Charge, Haddington.
340 Smith, Robert, 24 Meadowside, Dundee.
Smythe, David M., Methven Castle, Perth.
Sprott, Rev. George W., D.D., The Manse, North Berwick.
Stair, Earl of, Oxenfoord Castle, Dalkeith.
Steele, W. Cunninghame, Advocate, 21 Drummond Place, Edinburgh.
Stevenson, J. H., Advocate, 10 Albyn Place, Edinburgh.
Stevenson, Rev. Robert, M.A., The Abbey, Dunfermline.
Stevenson, T. G., 22 Frederick Street, Edinburgh.
Stevenson, William, Towerbank, Lenzie, by Glasgow.
Stewart, Donald W., 62 Princes Street, Edinburgh.
350 Stewart, Major-General Shaw, 61 Lancaster Gate, London, W.
Stewart, James R., 31 George Square, Edinburgh.
Stewart, R. K., Murdostoun Castle, Newmains, Lanarkshire.
Stewart, Prof. T. Grainger, M.D., 19 Charlotte Sq., Edinburgh.
Stirling, Major C. C. Graham, Craigbarnet, Haughhead of Campsie, Glasgow.
Strathallan, Lord, Carlton Club, Pall Mall, London, S.W.
Strathern, Robert, W.S., 12 South Charlotte St., Edinburgh.
Strathmore, Earl of, Glamis Castle, Glamis.
Stuart, Surgeon-Major G. B., 7 Carlton Street, Edinburgh.
Sturrock, James S., W.S., 110 George Street, Edinburgh.
360 Sutherland, James B., S.S.C., 10 Windsor Street, Edinburgh.

Taylor, Benjamin, 10 Derby Crescent, Kelvinside, Glasgow.
Taylor, Rev. Malcolm C., D.D., Professor of Church History, 6 Greenhill Park, Edinburgh.
Telford, Rev. W. H., Free Church Manse, Reston, Berwickshire.
Tennant, Sir Charles, Bart., The Glen, Innerleithen.
Thoms, George H. M., Advocate, 13 Charlotte Sq., Edinburgh.
Thomson, John Comrie, Advocate, 30 Moray Place, Edinburgh.
Thomson, Rev. John Henderson, Free Church Manse Hightae, by Lockerbie.

Thomson, John Maitland, Advocate, 18 Atholl Cres., Edinburgh.
Thomson, Lockhart, S.S.C., 114 George Street, Edinburgh.
370 Thorburn, Robert Macfie, Uddevalla, Sweden.
Trail, John A., LL.B., W.S., 30 Drummond Place, Edinburgh.
Trayner, The Hon. Lord, 27 Moray Place, Edinburgh.
Tuke, John Batty, M.D., 20 Charlotte Square, Edinburgh.
Tweedale, Mrs., Milton Hall, Milton, Cambridge.
Tweeddale, Marquis of, Yester, Gifford, Haddington.

UNDERHILL, CHARLES E., M.D., 8 Coates Crescent, Edinburgh.

VEITCH, Professor, LL.D., 4 The College, Glasgow.

WADDEL, ALEXANDER, Royal Bank, Calton, Glasgow.
Walker, Alexander, 64 Hamilton Place, Aberdeen.
380 Walker, James, Hanley Lodge, Corstorphine.
Walker, Louson, Westhorpe, Greenock.
Walker, Robert, M.A., University Library, Aberdeen.
Wannop, Rev. Canon, Parsonage, Haddington.
Watson, D., Hillside Cottage, Hawick.
Watson, James, Myskyns, Ticehurst, Hawkhurst.
Waugh, Alexander, National Bank, Newton-Stewart, N.B.
Weld-French, A. D., Union Club, Boston, U.S.
Wilson, Rev. J. Skinner, 4 Duke Street, Edinburgh.
Wilson, John J., Clydesdale Bank, Penicuik.
390 Wilson, Robert, Procurator-Fiscal, County Buildings, Hamilton.
Wilson, Robert Dobie, 38 Upper Brook Street, London.
Wood, Alexander, Thornly, Saltcoats.
Wood, Mrs. Christina S., Woodburn, Galashiels.
Wood, Prof. J. P., W.S., 16 Buckingham Terrace, Edinburgh.
Wood, W. A., C.A., 11 Clarendon Crescent, Edinburgh.
Wordie, John, 49 West Nile Street, Glasgow.

YOUNG, A. J., Advocate, 60 Great King Street, Edinburgh.
Young, David, Town Clerk, Paisley.
Young, J. W., W.S., 22 Royal Circus, Edinburgh.
400 Young, William Laurence, Solicitor, Auchterarder.

PUBLIC LIBRARIES.

Aberdeen Free Public Library.
Aberdeen University Library.
All Souls' College, Oxford.
Antiquaries, Society of, Edinburgh.
Baillie's Institution Free Library, 48 Miller St., Glasgow.
Belfast Library, Donegal Square, North, Ireland.
Berlin Royal Library.
Bodleian Library, Oxford.
Boston Athenæum.
10 Boston Public Library.
Cambridge University Library.
Copenhagen (Bibliothèque Royale).
Dollar Institution.
Dundee Free Library.
Dresden Public Library.
Edinburgh Public Library.
Edinburgh University Library.
Free Church College Library, Edinburgh.
Free Church College Library, Glasgow.
20 Glasgow University Library.
Gray's Inn, Hon. Society of, London.
Harvard College Library, Cambridge, Mass.
Leeds Subscription Library.
London Corporation Library, Guildhall.
London Library, 12 St. James Square.
Manchester Public Free Library.
Mitchell Library, Glasgow.
National Liberal Club, London.
National Library of Ireland.
30 Nottingham Free Public Library.
Ottawa Parliamentary Library.
Paisley Philosophical Institution.
Philosophical Institution, Edinburgh.
Procurators, Faculty of, Glasgow.
Reform Club, Pall Mall, London, S.W.
Royal College of Physicians, Edinburgh.
St. Andrews University Library.
Sheffield Free Public Library.
Signet Library, Edinburgh.
40 Solicitors, Society of, before the Supreme Court, Edinburgh.
Speculative Society, Edinburgh.
Stonyhurst College, Blackburn, Lancashire.
Sydney Free Library.
Vienna, Library of the R. I. University.

Scottish History Society.

THE EXECUTIVE.

President.
THE EARL OF ROSEBERY, K.G.

Chairman of Council.
DAVID MASSON, LL.D., Historiographer Royal for Scotland.

Council.
J. N. MACPHAIL, Advocate.
Rev. A. W. CORNELIUS HALLEN.
Sir ARTHUR MITCHELL, K.C.B., M.D., LL.D.
Rev. GEO. W. SPROTT, D.D.
J. BALFOUR PAUL, Lyon King of Arms.
A. H. MILLAR.
J. R. FINDLAY.
P. HUME BROWN, M.A.
G. GREGORY SMITH, M.A.
J. FERGUSON, Advocate.
Right Rev. JOHN DOWDEN, D.D., Bishop of Edinburgh.
ÆNEAS J. G. MACKAY, LL.D., Sheriff of Fife.

Corresponding Members of the Council.
C. H. FIRTH, Oxford ; SAMUEL RAWSON GARDINER, LL.D. ; Rev.
W. D. MACRAY, Oxford ; Rev. Professor A. F. MITCHELL, D.D.,
St. Andrews ; Professor J. VEITCH, LL.D., Glasgow.

Hon. Treasurer.
J. T. CLARK, Keeper of the Advocates' Library.

Hon. Secretary.
T. G. LAW, Librarian, Signet Library.

RULES

1. THE object of the Society is the discovery and printing, under selected editorship, of unpublished documents illustrative of the civil, religious, and social history of Scotland. The Society will also undertake, in exceptional cases, to issue translations of printed works of a similar nature, which have not hitherto been accessible in English.

2. The number of Members of the Society shall be limited to 400.

3. The affairs of the Society shall be managed by a Council, consisting of a Chairman, Treasurer, Secretary, and twelve elected Members, five to make a quorum. Three of the twelve elected Members shall retire annually by ballot, but they shall be eligible for re-election.

4. The Annual Subscription to the Society shall be One Guinea. The publications of the Society shall not be delivered to any Member whose Subscription is in arrear, and no Member shall be permitted to receive more than one copy of the Society's publications.

5. The Society will undertake the issue of its own publications, i.e. without the intervention of a publisher or any other paid agent.

6. The Society will issue yearly two octavo volumes of about 320 pages each.

7. An Annual General Meeting of the Society shall be held on the last Tuesday in October.

8. Two stated Meetings of the Council shall be held each year, one on the last Tuesday of May, the other on the Tuesday preceding t he day upon which the Annual General Meeting shall be held. The Secretary, on the request of three Members of the Council, shall call a special meeting of the Council.

9. Editors shall receive 20 copies of each volume they edit for the Society.

10. The owners of Manuscripts published by the Society will also be presented with a certain number of copies.

11. The Annual Balance-Sheet, Rules, and List of Members shall be printed.

12. No alteration shall be made in these Rules except at a General Meeting of the Society. A fortnight's notice of any alteration to be proposed shall be given to the Members of the Council.

PUBLICATIONS

OF THE

SCOTTISH HISTORY SOCIETY

For the year 1886-1887.

1. BISHOP POCOCKE'S TOURS IN SCOTLAND, 1747-1760.   Edited by
   D. W. KEMP.   (Oct. 1887.)

2. DIARY OF AND GENERAL EXPENDITURE BOOK OF WILLIAM
   CUNNINGHAM OF CRAIGENDS, 1673-1680.   Edited by the Rev.
   JAMES DODDS, D.D.   (Oct. 1887.)

For the year 1887-1888.

3. PANURGI PHILO-CABALLI SCOTI GRAMEIDOS LIBRI SEX. — THE
   GRAMEID: an heroic poem descriptive of the Campaign of
   Viscount Dundee in 1689, by JAMES PHILIP of Almerieclose.
   Translated and Edited by the Rev. A. D. MURDOCH.
                                                       (Oct. 1888.)

4. THE REGISTER OF THE KIRK-SESSION OF ST. ANDREWS.   Part I.
   1559-1582.   Edited by D. HAY FLEMING.   (Feb. 1889.)

For the year 1888-1889.

5. DIARY OF THE REV. JOHN MILL, Minister of Dunrossness, Sand-
   wick, and Cunningsburgh, in Shetland, 1740-1803.   Edited
   by GILBERT GOUDIE, F.S.A. Scot.   (June 1889.)

6. NARRATIVE OF MR. JAMES NIMMO, A COVENANTER, 1654-1709.
   Edited by W. G. SCOTT-MONCRIEFF, Advocate.   (June 1889.)

7. THE REGISTER OF THE KIRK-SESSION OF ST. ANDREWS.   Part II.
   1583-1600.   Edited by D. HAY FLEMING.   (Aug. 1890.)

For the year 1889-1890.

8. A LIST OF PERSONS CONCERNED IN THE REBELLION (1745). With a Preface by the EARL OF ROSEBERY and Annotations by the Rev. WALTER MACLEOD. (Sept. 1890.)

Presented to the Society by the Earl of Rosebery.

9. GLAMIS PAPERS: The 'BOOK OF RECORD,' a Diary written by PATRICK, FIRST EARL OF STRATHMORE, and other documents relating to Glamis Castle (1684-89). Edited by A. H. MILLAR, F.S.A. Scot. (Sept. 1890.)

10. JOHN MAJOR'S HISTORY OF GREATER BRITAIN (1521). Translated and Edited by ARCHIBALD CONSTABLE, with a Life of the author by ÆNEAS J. G. MACKAY, Advocate. (Feb. 1892.)

For the year 1890-1891.

11. THE RECORDS OF THE COMMISSIONS OF THE GENERAL ASSEMBLIES, 1646-47. Edited by the Rev. Professor MITCHELL, D.D., and the Rev. JAMES CHRISTIE, D.D., with an Introduction by the former. (May 1892.)

12. COURT-BOOK OF THE BARONY OF URIE, 1604-1747. Edited by the Rev. D. G. BARRON, from a MS. in possession of Mr. R. BARCLAY of Dorking. (Oct. 1892.)

For the year 1891-1892.

13. MEMOIRS OF THE LIFE OF SIR JOHN CLERK OF PENICUIK, Baronet, Baron of the Exchequer, Commissioner of the Union, etc. Extracted by himself from his own Journals, 1676-1755. Edited from the original MS. in Penicuik House by JOHN M. GRAY, F.S.A. Scot. (Dec. 1892.)

14. DIARY OF COL. THE HON. JOHN ERSKINE OF CARNOCK, 1683-1687. From a MS. in possession of HENRY DAVID ERSKINE, Esq., of Cardross. Edited by the Rev. WALTER MACLEOD. (Dec. 1893.)

For the year 1892-1893.

15. Miscellany of the Scottish History Society, First Volume—

The Library of James vi., 1573-83, edited by G. F. Warner.

Documents illustrating Catholic Policy, 1596-98, edited by T. G. Law.

Letters of Sir Thomas Hope, 1627-46, edited by the Rev. Robert Paul.

Civil War Papers, 1645-50, edited by H. F. Morland Simpson.

Lauderdale Correspondence, 1660-77, edited by the Right Rev. Bishop Dowden.

Turnbull's Diary, 1657-1704, edited by the Rev. R. Paul.

Masterton Papers, 1660-1719, edited by V. A. Noël Paton.

Accompt of Expenses in Edinburgh, 1715, edited by A. H. Millar.

Rebellion Papers, 1715 and 1745, edited by Henry Paton.
(Dec. 1893.)

16. Account Book of Sir John Foulis of Ravelston (1671-1707). Edited by the Rev. A. W. Cornelius Hallen.
(*Nearly ready.*)

For the year 1893-1894.

The Jacobite Rising of 1719. Letter Book of James, Second Duke of Ormonde, Nov. 4, 1718—Sept. 27, 1719. Edited by John Russell. (*In progress.*)

Charles ii. and the Marquis of Montrose, 1651. Edited by Samuel Rawson Gardiner. (*In progress.*)

Papers relating to the Military Occupation of Scotland by General Monk and the Government of Robert Lilburne, 1651-1654. Edited by C. H. Firth.

In preparation.

Records of the Commissions of the General Assemblies (*continued*) for the years 1648-49, 1649-50, 1651-52. Edited by the Rev. Professor Mitchell and Rev. James Christie.

SIR THOMAS CRAIG'S DE UNIONE REGNORUM BRITANNIÆ. Edited, with an English Translation, from the unpublished manuscript in the Advocates' Library, by DAVID MASSON, Historiographer Royal.

THE DIARY OF ANDREW HAY OF STONE, NEAR BIGGAR, AFTERWARDS OF CRAIGNETHAN CASTLE, 1659-60. Edited by A. G. REID from a manuscript in his possession.

THE LYON IN MOURNING : FORBES' MEMOIRS OF THE REBELLION OF 1745. Edited from the original in the Advocates' Library by HENRY PATON.

A TRANSLATION OF THE STATUTA ECCLESIÆ SCOTICANÆ, 1225-1556, by DAVID PATRICK.

A TRANSLATION OF THE HISTORIA ABBATUM DE KYNLOS OF FERRERIUS, by ARCHIBALD CONSTABLE.

A SELECTION OF THE FORFEITED ESTATES PAPERS PRESERVED IN H.M. GENERAL REGISTER HOUSE. Edited by A. H. MILLAR.

DOCUMENTS IN THE ARCHIVES OF HOLLAND CONCERNING THE SCOTS DUTCH BRIGADE AND CHURCHES.

DOCUMENTS RELATING TO THE AFFAIRS OF THE ROMAN CATHOLIC PARTY IN SCOTLAND, from the year of the Armada to the Union of the Crowns. Edited by THOMAS GRAVES LAW.

www.ingramcontent.com/pod-product-compliance
Lightning Source LLC
Chambersburg PA
CBHW020336090426
42735CB00009B/1560